KV-576-469

Citizen of Zimbabwe

Citizen of Zimbabwe
Conversations with Morgan Tsvangirai

Stephen Chan

WEAVER PRESS

Weaver Press
P O Box A1922
Avondale, Harare
Zimbabwe
www.weaverpresszimbabwe.com

Second edition, 2010
First published in a private edition in 2005

All rights reserved

No part of this book may be reproduced in any form,
or by electronic or mechanical means, including information storage
or retrieval systems, without permission in writing
from the publishers, except by a reviewer
who may quote brief passages in a review.

© Stephen Chan 2005, 2010

Cover: Danes Design, Harare
© Cover photo: Office of the Prime Minister, Harare
Typeset by forzalibro designs, Cape Town
Printed and bound in Zimbabwe by
Sable Press, Harare

ISBN 978-1-77922-105-6

WEAVER
W
–PRESS–

Contents

Contents

Preface to the Second Edition

The first edition of this book, *Citizen of Africa: Conversations with Morgan Tsvangirai*, was written in late 2004, after protracted interviews in Harare with Morgan Tsvangirai, and was released as an 'underground' or *samizdat* edition for the elections of 2005. It bore no publisher's imprint or ISBN, and was distributed by the MDC as part of its press pack to visiting observers, journalists, scholars and the assorted hangers-on that are the paraphernalia and travelling circus at any election – never mind one in the troubled Zimbabwe of that year. I attended those elections, as I have most Zimbabwean elections, including both rounds of those in 2008. But, in 2005, the government's efforts to massage a sort of calm in the fortnight before polling beguiled several foreign observers, many of whom never moved far from Harare. And, indeed, despite having been involved in the pioneering Commonwealth Observer Group in Zimbabwe in 1980, I have long doubted the efficacy not of observers, but of the observation process as currently practiced. It has not, in official circles, moved on from 1980, and I shall write about that in the future.

It seemed time for an 'above ground' edition for three reasons. Firstly, an unauthorised or 'pirate' edition was released, not in China where I expected, but in the United States. It had an ISBN, and many American university and other libraries purchased it before I threatened the publishers with legal action. But there seemed a hunger to read or reference the book. Secondly, it has become a curious collector's item, selling for up to $500 on the international web markets; and I really am not sure I want Zimbabwean political developments to be the property of connoisseurs; and thirdly, of course, Morgan Tsvangirai is now Prime Minister and it really is about time that all of Zimbabwean society, together with its curious artefacts – like this book – came above ground and entered as open a debate as any difficult moment in history deserves.

Weaver Press were the originators of the underground edition, and I thank them for their support and for the risks they took. Ranka Primorac is a source of both knowledge and critical opinion. I thank her for all she brings. My many friends in Zimbabwe, and in the South Africa which brokered the power-sharing deal in Zimbabwe, will know how indebted I am to them. Even now, I don't want to name them but, one day, when the country really has attained its place of decency, there will have to be the party of all time.

London, 2010.

Introduction

The idea for this book came at Easter 2004. At that time the ruling party in Zimbabwe, ZANU(PF), thought it had turned a corner in its struggle with the opposition MDC. On 29 March the MDC had lost the parliamentary by-election in Zengeza – a seat it would normally have regarded as a stronghold. There had been no massive intimidation of voters by ZANU(PF),[1] but the four years of continuing harassment since the MDC won the 2000 constitutional referendum – a war of unremitting attrition – had taken their toll. The MDC was demoralised. Its tactics of resistance, mass days of urban action, strikes and stayaways, had not led to the crumbling of ZANU(PF). In fact, ZANU(PF) did not even seem weakened. Nevertheless, the defeat at Zengeza revitalised the debate within the MDC as to whether it should boycott the parliamentary elections in March 2005. A triumphant Robert Mugabe mocked his defeated opponents:

> They now fear elections and are giving all sorts of lame excuses for boycotting elections. We dare them. Boycott or no boycott, well, you are ripe for burial and we will put you to eternal sleep in March next year, but not at the Heroes Acre.[2]

A string of articles in the state press appeared, with very little variation, pronouncing upon the decline and imminent demise of the MDC. Some of this played upon emerging factions within the opposition. One headline, 'MDC intellectuals plan splinter party',[3] was particularly revealing, as if ZANU(PF) discerned an Achilles' Heel within the MDC – the uneasy alliance between trade unionists and their days of action, and their more cerebral colleagues who had become alarmed at the MDC's lack of skilful representation both at home and abroad. Even the residual non-government press, down to three weeklies after the government had successfully pushed the *Daily News* into closure, was unflattering of the MDC and its prospects. The headline, 'Is MDC's urban support on the wane?',[4] merely repeated a question on everyone's lips. And two headlines in the *Financial Gazette*, the longest-surviving independent newspaper, suggested that the 'MDC

1

for complacency' and, more ominously, sought to analyse '[t]he leadership cancer in the MDC'.[5]

None of this should, however, underestimate the campaign waged by ZANU(PF) against the MDC; nor should it underestimate the huge disparity in the organisational foundations of the two parties. The government could pour huge resources into ZANU(PF). It monopolised all broadcasting. The press, whether free or not, was only a minor player compared to the rural outreach of indigenous-language radio. The MDC had initially organised well in its urban heartlands, but had no real rural infrastructure – and neither its trade unionists nor its intellectuals had any sustained sense of rural policy. ZANU(PF), on the other hand, had built a formidable party control of the countryside, which in more recent days it had augmented with paramilitary bullying and control of food relief. Its farm seizures had caused chaos, dislocation and hunger. Equitable land redistribution was always going to be necessary in an independent Zimbabwe; however, the manner in which the process has been carried out and the distribution of land to a chosen elite have rendered the process violent and unjust. With its rural control mechanisms, and a sullen but not seriously resistant acquiescence to its policies, ZANU(PF) continued to command most of the countryside while the MDC searched for a viable urban strategy. And, even in the MDC urban strongholds, ZANU(PF) militants often had free rein to bully, beat and intimidate all those they suspected of opposition membership. They are dramatic parallels, but I have always likened the MDC's efforts to those of the horse-mounted Polish and Finnish cavalry units who heroically charged the armoured tanks of Hitler on the one hand and Stalin on the other; or of the Bangladeshi farmers who, mounted on tractors, charged against a squadron of Pakistani tanks. The Poles, Finns and Bangladeshis all won in the end – but after much time and cost. In Zimbabwe, it seemed the MDC was arguing over what sort of sabre should be used against the ZANU(PF) tanks. And ZANU(PF), having first ensured it would maintain the disparities in strength, was crowing. The loss of Zengeza was followed by others, and these were dark days for the MDC.

There is a tendency within Zimbabwe – not unlike that in many developing countries – to view politics through largely local lenses. The outside world is curiously over-interpreted (as if, for example, the West monopolised the flow of capital, whereas it is capital that drives the West as much as the developing world) and under-interpreted (as if, for example, the West should see Zimbabwean issues in Zimbabwean terms). The complex ground between these two broad analyses – perhaps they are assumptions upon which analyses may be built – tends to be under-appreciated. Both ZANU(PF) and the MDC have a tendency to engage in this localising of politics. However, although fully conscious it was alienating the West through its land-seizure policies, ZANU(PF) and particularly Robert Mugabe went out of their way to build a pan-African support-base. It was so successful that neither Britain nor the US, and not even France with its close ties to a large part of Africa, could fully isolate Zimbabwe from its Africa-wide support. This diplomatic achievement – for that is what it was – was established upon a curious intellectualism: that Africa was in the midst of developing its own forms of reasoning and political rationality and, even if democracy and freedom were agreed as real or aspirant values, the institutions to further African democracy and freedom were an African affair and should not be imposed by the West. Its seeking to do so was one further example of a neo-imperialism, if not racism, that Africa was best advised to resist. This sort of generalised reasoning accounts for the large support ZANU(PF) continues to enjoy from many Zimbabwean academics. It underpinned the rhetoric and much of the strategic direction of Jonathan Moyo, Mugabe's ex-cabinet intellectual – however opportunistic and ruthless his tactics may have been. And it underpins Thabo Mbeki's reluctance to condemn Mugabe – lest he be condemned in turn for being an instrument of the West. In one of Mbeki's newsletters to the ANC – and these are published and read widely throughout Africa – Mbeki cited the Kenyan novelist, Ngugi wa Thiongo, and his book *Decolonising the Mind* – although it was clear Mbeki had not read all the nuances of that book. Mbeki repeated its often vulgarised message that it was time for Africans to think their way forward in an original African way.[6] The interesting thing was that Mbeki was using an intellectual source to protest the seeming railroading of Zimbabwe's suspension from the Commonwealth at the Abuja summit on 7 December 2003. Mbeki can still be pragmatic and, above all, patient but his intellectual roots are not hidden.

If the MDC was extremely happy about the Abuja result it was not because it had brought it about. The MDC was only a side-player at Abuja and, even at the March 2002 Commonwealth summit in Brisbane, where the suspension of Zimbabwe was first mooted, the MDC delegation was noted for its lack of diplomatic skill. Making party speeches that would have gone down well at political rallies is not an ideal approach to more than 50 world leaders. I have written elsewhere that, at Abuja, both the British and the Commonwealth Secretary-General conspicuously failed to appreciate the intellectual underpinning of the broad African position on Zimbabwe.[7] But, even before Brisbane, when the MDC should have been refining its Commonwealth strategy, the MDC's then-spokesman for foreign affairs, Tendai Biti, in a conversation with me, seemed to accord the summit little value. 'Morgan has not yet decided whether he will attend the Brisbane summit.'[8] My conversations with Tsvangirai himself, a year earlier in October 2000, had shown a pungent honesty about international affairs – but also a naivety:

> *We really have to redefine the Commonwealth role. I really don't know how relevant it can be to contemporary needs – especially the fact that it is comprised by ex-British colonies rather distances itself from what I see as our contemporary realities. I'll be in London on the 5th and 6th of November, and I might or might not – I'm not sure – whether I'll see the Commonwealth Secretary-General, Don McKinnon. You know, such men want the best of both worlds. They're unaware of realities on the ground, and think a few passing, choice words will still suffice. McKinnon simply has not been strong enough in the face of Mugabe's antics...*
>
> *The Harare Declaration* [on human rights], *ah ha, you know this is the saddest thing about Africa, all these flowery declarations and all without commitment. There's no commitment because there is no holding to account. They are not held to account in international relations, the leaders who make these flowery declarations. They feel no responsibility to the declarations but, more, they feel no responsibility to ethical standards, to any ethical philosophy. The declarations are not worth the paper they're written on. Releasing such paper creates a feel-good atmosphere and, when leaders are reminded of what they have signed, they, ha, retreat into the defence of the sovereignty of nations.[9]*

As it turned out, the Commonwealth did – finally and with great difficulty – hold Zimbabwe to account, and used the Harare Declaration to do so. The point is that, although everything Tsvangirai said is in a bald sense true, this is the crude ground on which diplomacy sits. What the MDC position should have been was a strategic outreach to people such as McKinnon to work together towards a holding to account. McKinnon was hardly beloved of Mugabe either; but the MDC missed the opportunity to strategically engage with Britain through the diplomatic channels of the Commonwealth. In short, among the Commonwealth Heads of Government, Tsvangirai did not look like a Head of Government.

By that time, Tsvangirai had been charged with treason (25 February 2002) on account of a secretly-filmed video of his conferring with Ari Ben-Manashe – who turned out to be in Mugabe's pay – in which Tsvangirai had talked about the 'elimination' of Mugabe. It has been seen as a ZANU(PF) master-class in entrapment, but in that case it also showed the inexperience and shallowness of the MDC in international circles. Ben-Manashe was hardly unknown and, from what was known, the MDC would have been well advised to steer very clear of him. The episode caused the Zimbabwean courts to embargo any further overseas travel for Tsvangirai. However naive his early efforts at international diplomacy had been, Tsvangirai was now not going to be able to practise and make it better. He could no longer travel to see McKinnon even if he wanted to. And those coming in to see him would be easily monitored.

One of the reasons for this present book is to see what sort of older and wiser leader Tsvangirai now is. All the pressures on him, and all the ZANU(PF) entrapments and constraints, harassment and capacity for crowing have not stopped him. He is certainly dogged and persistent. But he might also have learnt under fire. Pressure-cooking can sometimes lead to unexpected results. So is Tsvangirai still merely a charismatic leader of the opposition? In trying to cast him down, what might ZANU(PF) have raised up?

The second reason is precisely related to the point made above, that an intellectual agenda has been set. This is not only to do with ownership of power and ownership of land, but ownership of what ZANU(PF) has called 'patriotic history'. Terence Ranger has discussed this.[10] Ian Phimister and Brian Raftopoulos have also, stressing that the ZANU(PF) ideological project is complex, that it has repercussions and echoes throughout Africa.[11] Perhaps the Zimbabwean case is itself the echo of something not yet fully choate but which is striving to articulate itself in the continent and has caught the admiration of much African opinion. Even shorn of an ideology of anti-imperialism, there is still a project to do – for the first time – with an autonomous African philosophy. Senghor, Nkrumah, Nyerere and Kaunda all tried before to suggest such a philosophy – but failed.[12] The desire for autonomy, for genuine intellectual decolonisation, seeps into the foreign policies of Africa to an extent that the Blairs of the world have never suspected (and the French have grudgingly come to accept). So the second reason for this book is to look, for the first time, at whether Morgan Tsvangirai has his own intellectual agenda, his own thought base, a political philosophy; something perhaps that transcends the much advertised split within the MDC between trade unionists and intellectuals.

I did not want to approach this book in anything but an even-handed manner. The book is not a tract. Indeed, I wanted to approach Tsvangirai as I had approached Mugabe. My book on Mugabe was both criticised and praised for being even-handed. Unlike my Mugabe book, however, the present work will not be an academic one; and even the Mugabe book trod a fine line between an academically-based work and one accessible to the general public.

This present book is being written in August 2004. The aim is that it should be available before the March 2005 parliamentary elections in Zimbabwe. At the time of writing, almost all the diplomatic opinion in the Harare embassies and at ministerial level in Whitehall is it, should the elections be contested by the MDC, ZANU(PF) will win – even without rigging (although whether it can resist rigging is another question). Expert opinion is that the MDC is factionalised, demoralised, and that the pressures on Tsvangirai – with the possibility of a guilty verdict in his treason trial hanging over him – have kept him on the back foot. By contrast, ZANU(PF) seems resurgent in its confidence. The new Governor of the Reserve Bank of Zimbabwe had partially and modestly stabilised the economy near the end of 2004, although at a very low level and followed by instability at the start of 2005, giving the lie to assertions that Zimbabwe's economic woes have bottomed-out. If the MDC not only loses, but loses its blocking vote in Parliament (where ZANU(PF) requires a two-thirds majority to change the Constitution), then effective opposition to the Mugabe regime will be, to all intents and purposes, over. The idea behind rushing this book into the public eye is so that, if the political career of Morgan Tsvangirai is also then over, at least an extended account of what he stands for and thinks about will have been made available. But who knows?

I have been following the career of Morgan Tsvangirai since its trade union inception. For the sake of this book he agreed to talk extensively with me, and these discussions took place towards the end of July 2004. Except where indicated, all quotes from Tsvangirai are taken from these discussions. About a week before I left London it was announced that the verdict of Tsvangirai's treason trial would be released on 29 July. A welter of conflicting thoughts came to my head. Opportunistic: if he were found guilty, would I have possibly the last interview with him? Concern for friends: if he were found guilty, would Harare erupt into flames? And others. But the ticket was non-refundable, and I wanted to be there if history was made.

I was greatly shamed by Morgan Tsvangirai. The verdict was postponed shortly before my arrival, and one of our discussion days coincided with 29 July. On a day when he could easily have been sentenced to a hangman's noose he was cordiality and openness personified – calm as ice. I want to say at the outset that I was greatly impressed. Whatever people have said in the past about his technical capacities to be President, he has the character to be President. This will emerge in the book ahead. But perhaps that is one of the reasons why Robert Mugabe and ZANU(PF), in their heavy-handed way, have taken him so seriously.

Notes

1. This is a contentious judgement, but was supported by all the diplomatic opinion
   I canvassed during my visit to Zimbabwe at that time. This included high-level

Western diplomatic sources, representing governments hardly beloved of Mr Mugabe and ZANU(PF).

2. *The Saturday Herald* (Harare), 3 April 2004, p. 1.
3. *The Sunday Mail* (Harare), 4 April 2004, p. 3.
4. *The Standard* (Harare), 4 April 2004, p. 4.
5. *Financial Gazette* (Harare), 1-7 April 2004, p. 5 and p. 13.
6. Thabo Mbeki. 'We'll resist the upside-down view of Africa', *The Post* (Lusaka), 9 January 2004; Ngugi wa Thiongo, *Decolonising the Mind: The Politics of Language in African Literature* (Zimbabwean edition), Harare: Zimbabwe Publishing House, 1987.
7. Stephen Chan, 'Abuja and After: The Case for Change in the Commonwealth Secretariat', *The Round Table*, 374, 2004.
8. Author's interview with Tendai Biti, Harare, 24 August 2001 and 27 August 2001.
9. Author's interview with Morgan Tsvangirai, 23 and 24 October 2000, cited in Stephen Chan, 'Commonwealth Residualism and the Machinations of Power in a Turbulent Zimbabwe', *Commonwealth and Comparative Politics*, 39:3, 2001, p. 71.
10. Terence Ranger, 'Nationalist Historiography, Patriotic History and the History of the Nation: the Struggle over the Past in Zimbabwe', *Journal of Southern African Studies*, 30:2, 2004. A version of this article appears as a chapter in Robert Muponde and Ranka Primorac (eds), *Versions of Zimbabwe; Literature, History and Politics*, Harare: Weaver Press, 2005.
11. Ian Phimister and Brian Raftopoulos, 'Mugabe, Mbeki and the Politics of Anti-Imperialism', in *Review of African Political Economy*, 2004, v. 31, 385-400.
12. For my efforts to decipher Kaunda's philosophy, as applied to foreign policy, see Stephen Chan, *Kaunda and Southern Africa: Image and Reality in Foreign Policy*, London: I.B. Tauris, 1992.

A Short History

Morgan Tsvangirai's house is a comfortably sprawling single-story building in Strathaven, about five minutes' drive north-west of downtown Harare. It is, as are all houses in what are called 'low density' areas, surrounded by high walls. It is the counterpart designation of what are politely called 'high density' areas – meaning the poorer parts of town. Strathaven is not elite, but sufficiently middle-class for the houses to have not only walls but guards. Tsvangirai needs guards for different reasons to those of his neighbours, but his are well-dressed – they are MDC members and not uniformed security – and appallingly polite. I wonder what they have been through. Two weeks before we met, Tsvangirai and his party had been attacked by ZANU(PF) militants wielding axes – but, where the guards sit behind the gates to Tsvangirai's house and garden, there is not a weapon in sight.

The garden is beautiful, the lawns mowed, the hedges clipped – almost topiarised – and tall trees grow amidst the flowerbeds. A haven indeed. It is, it seems this very day, the end of the Harare winter. By local standards it has been a cold year. The tall flowering trees are beginning to produce pollen. One in particular gives Tsvangirai hay fever. He is suffering terribly, eyes red, having to blow his nose occasionally, but he cannot bring himself to cut down the tree. Tsvangirai has a deep interest in ecology. The troublesome tree is destined to survive a long time. We sit in his book-lined study in an annex to the main building. We begin our conversations with him seated behind a desk, but he migrates to the armchair beside me. *The Daily Telegraph* correspondent, Peta Thornycroft, comes to call and Tsvangirai introduces me as 'the man who wrote that book about Mugabe.' I reply, 'and in which I was very critical of you too.' He laughs and says, 'that was good, it meant the book was fair and objective.' He's read the book. He seems to read avariciously every title on Zimbabwe. Creased open on his desk is Luise White's latest work, *The Assassination of Herbert Chitepo.*[1] The shelves are filled mostly with Zimbabwean books. There does not appear anything by way of fiction. Morgan Tsvangirai does not seem to have the time for recreational reading. But our time on the first day passes pleasantly. He is a good interviewee, and I am myself becoming relaxed about the process. It is only when I cadge a ride back downtown in his wife's red utility van that I notice that it is lined with a neatly cut and fitted, but distinctly home-made, armour. It wouldn't stop much: rounds from a handgun, shrapnel from a distance. I don't think it would stop sustained AK fire, and certainly nothing stronger. The driver, one of the guards I met earlier, sees me musing and smiles. 'Better than nothing,' he says. He may not be armed, but the young man has sangfroid.

Morgan Tsvangirai's mother has come to the city to be with her son at the moment of the treason verdict. She replies to my greeting in Shona, having no English herself. I think of how the old woman would have followed the courtroom proceedings. She is on the verandah with Tsvangirai's mother-in-law, both sitting flat without chairs or stools, a curiously village scene in low-density Strathaven. And, of course, they are a reminder of the risks involved in being Morgan Tsvangirai – the family gathering itself in support, firstly of him, and if it all goes wrong, of one another. I drive away and the garden gates bolt shut behind me.

Morgan Tsvangirai was born in 1952 in Buhera in the east of Zimbabwe, the eldest son of a bricklayer. He left secondary school to become a textile weaver, then worked in a mine in Bindura, north-east of Harare. It was there that he became involved in union work, rising to become leader of the mining union. It was not until the late 1980s that he became head of the Zimbabwe Congress of Trade Unions (ZCTU) and gained a national platform. He is thus 28 years younger than Robert Mugabe, who has five university degrees, some earned by distance-education in prison. Tsvangirai did not participate in the liberation struggle and, indeed, the ZCTU was only able to be formed after independence had been gained. He was only 28 when independence came, 30 when the slaughters in Matabeleland began, and he became head of the ZCTU at about the same time as the ZANU(PF) renegade, Edgar Tekere, launched the first nationwide (but unsuccessful) electoral challenge to Mugabe.[2] Tsvangirai did not enter politics proper until a decade later, and thus is seen as a latecomer and, by ZANU(PF), as the inheritor of the fruits of independence rather than its progenitor.

Senior military personnel, in an ostentatious show of support for Mugabe before the 2002 Presidential elections, vowed they would never serve under anyone who had not himself fought for independence. But this was more than mere ostentation and rhetoric. The idea of a liberation government is strong. It is a government that, after years of colonial or minority rule, seized back power for the majority. This provides a further affinity between ZANU(PF) and the ANC of South

Africa: both see themselves as the successful victors in a liberation struggle – even though, in both cases, negotiation was finally as important as violent struggle. However, given the immense scar that colonialism and minority rule has left in Africa, the organisation required and the pride secured in struggle have meant, at the very least, that someone like Morgan Tsvangirai has come to politics without pedigree.

Tsvangirai has also been at odds with the nation's intellectuals. Long before the MDC, with its own 'intellectual faction', was formed, he wrote that 'Zimbabwe has the misfortune of producing so-called progressive intellectuals who have the habit of lecturing workers and peasants through journals published from their mansions in low-density suburbs.'[3] This early striving for a populist touch meant that later coalition-building, and holding disparate forces together in one opposition party, would prove to be difficult tasks.

Even so, life as an African trade union supremo at the beginning of the 1990s would have been exciting. Tsvangirai would have seen, in 1991, how his exact counterpart, Frederick Chiluba, in neighbouring Zambia, swept another founding father with liberation credentials from power. The fall of Kaunda was unprecedented in Africa.[4] But it followed closely the defeat of communist leaderships all over Europe, epitomised by the fall of the Berlin Wall in 1989. And there was change brewing in South Africa too. It was as if a new Zeitgeist was not only sweeping Europe, the home of colonialism, but might sweep those once colonised in Africa. Perhaps a second-generation age after independence might be possible. Whether Morgan Tsvangirai thought these things or not, he had his hands full with trade union business. Economic structural adjustment in the 1990s meant increasing hardships for the workforce. The trade unions had to fight not only to represent their members but also to avoid marginalisation in a hardball economic climate where negotiations were hardly welcome, and hardly possible, from the point of view of the economic adjusters, walking a tightrope between Harare and the World Bank and IMF in Washington.

The old Southern Rhodesia had a more extensive industrial base than many of its neighbours and, as a result, a history of organised labour. Labour and nationalist leaders were themselves not often given to free and democratic expression by those in the ranks; and members of organised labour valued the social and localised political bonds of union membership more than the larger nationalist struggle – which is precisely why, in the 1970s, the nationalist parties took their struggle into the bush.[5]

By the time of the Lancaster House talks over the independence of Zimbabwe, the unions were weak and had no say in the negotiations or the process of transition. Because the ZCTU was subsequently created by the newly independent government, it was dominated by government for most of the first decade of independence. It was only with the emergence of a new Secretary-General, Morgan Tsvangirai, in 1988 that the prospect of a truly autonomous labour movement was made possible. Even so, as Lloyd Sachikonye points out, the initial agenda of the ZCTU was fraught. It involved a struggle not only with employers and government, but government's adherence to an economic structural adjustment programme (ESAP) designed to accommodate the conditionalities imposed by the World Bank and IMF. Precisely because of ESAP, the unions had to make some choices of priority: wage demands or employment security. Both wages and job security were threatened by ESAP, and the unions had to learn to negotiate on a variety of fronts, with individual employers as much as government. Moreover, union management was weak and membership was uneven. Eighty-three per cent of all parastatal workers were unionised, but the figures were much less in other sectors. Workers in the public sector had been excluded from unionisation.[6] And, more to the point of later events, effective unionisation of farm workers was never achieved.[7] In a study completed just before Tsvangirai became ZCTU Secretary-General – a rare, extended in-depth survey by a non-Zimbabwean, and possibly still the only such survey of its kind – Jeffrey Herbst was simply scathing of the early ZCTU. It was 'poorly organised', and its 'ability to learn was so poor' that its effect was, if not marginal, able to be marginalised.[8] What Tsvangirai did with the trade union movement was, given its history and condition, nothing short of remarkable. He established considerable leadership credentials throughout the 1990s.

The first high point of the new ZCTU style was controversial. Many, nostalgic for a mythological trade union socialism, see what occurred as a selling-out, an acceptance of liberalism and its ills. However, the ZCTU document of 1996, *Beyond ESAP*, prepared on the eve of structural adjustment's second round, was staggering when compared to the poor 'ability to learn' so recently described by Herbst. This was a document towards 'bargained liberalisation', an attempt to 'engage the state and capital in institutional structures which would be used to set the form and pace of adjustment.' The new approach was to 'shift the debate from a political level to a more strictly technical/economic one of issues requiring state interventions, within a social democratic framework.'[9] The extent to which Tsvangirai was involved in the writing of this document is unclear. The key point is that he sanctioned and encouraged it, and was prepared to negotiate on the basis of it. The political impact of advancing a technocratic document, and the knowledge that for the past year the ZCTU had been moving towards a technocratic dimension, was immediate. In 1995 Mugabe attended the May Day celebrations for the first time since 1991. The ZCTU, in urn, did not become involved in either the parliamentary election of)5 or the Presidential election of 1996. The document is certainly, even now, a signal to the outside world of a certain pragmatism in economic affairs – though couched in a social democratic idealism – that illustrates the Tsvangirai position. It also further illustrates why certain Zimbabwean intellectuals, imbued with neo-Marxist critiques of the world economy, see Tsvangirai as inimical to their sense of historical progress – although these same critics have never yet reconciled the antipathy in their intellectual goals, with an African philosophical and ideological autonomy on the one hand, and an international socialism on the other. The two can be made to fit, but only with artifice and lack of complicating detail. The sheer realism of *Beyond ESAP* remains a model in Zimbabwean politics.

As late as the mid-1990s, then, Tsvangirai and Mugabe were able to co-operate. Tsvangirai has made no secret of his early and long-standing admiration of Mugabe. It was only at this point, coming into very recent history, that the wheel began to turn. In 1996, public sector workers, led by teachers and nurses, went on strike. Previously uninvolved with such workers, the ZCTU now affiliated them. It should be said that, even here, the ZCTU was a stabilising and moderating device – but it now had a huge swathe of urban workers in its fold and, more tellingly, the public sector workers represented a dissatisfaction at the coalface of government policy implementation. The ZCTU was becoming both larger and more politicised; and this may not have been inexorable but for what happened in 1997. What happened then would assemble the complete cast for the events from 2000 onwards.

In 1997, the Zimbabwe National Liberation War Veterans' Association led by Chenjerai Hunzvi – a Polish-trained physician who was not himself a veteran – intensified its lobbying for higher financial benefits. Most veterans had not benefited from independence, despite being the frontline fighters for it; nor had they been properly compensated for the suffering and hardships they had endured. It was the advent of Hunzvi that allowed the veterans to organise themselves better and lobby more effectively than before. Their demands received such publicity that it became impossible for Mugabe, the 'father of liberation', to ignore the liberators. Giving in to a political demand meant, however, a demand on the economy. Mugabe agreed to make a lump-sum compensation of Z$50,000 to each veteran, with an assured monthly pension thereafter. The national budget, still reeling from the effects of the public sector strike, and tightened to the point of inflexibility under ESAP, couldn't cope. Mugabe proposed a levy on all workers to pay the bill and, of course, the ZCTU resisted this. Tsvangirai and Hunzvi did meet to explore other means of financing the gains of the veterans, but this came to nothing.[10] Moreover, if it came to a choice between the ZCTU and the veterans, Mugabe would choose to side with the veterans. Not wishing, however, to alienate either at first, Mugabe dropped the levy while insisting the payments would go ahead. The economic result was massive. International financial institutions criticised the government's policy. A huge devaluation took place, inflation and the cost of living began to rise dramatically. On 9 December 1997, the most comprehensive national strike in Zimbabwean (and Rhodesian) history took place. Organised by the ZCTU, the grievance was now not only about fair economic benefits for workers but about the handling of the economy and, not far from explicitly, the fairness and capacity of the government itself. From 19 to 21 January 1998, urban riots broke out – and the complaint of the rioters was very much against the government and against Mugabe himself. While the ZCTU was not behind these riots, it now knew that it had national muscle that it could flex.

Drawing battlelines

The December 1997 strike involved the entire country but, without a rural support base, the ZCTU was prone to the charge of support from white Zimbabweans and, though not necessarily a logical corollary, the charge of support from white commercial farmers in particular. The Minister of Home Affairs said it had been 'an unholy alliance between the ZCTU, employers and white commercial farmers.'[11] And, in the wake of the January riots, Mugabe warned, 'the freedom that you have came from the people, from ZANU(PF) and those who chose to fight while you stayed behind enjoying everyday comforts' – a pointed attack on Tsvangirai's non-participation in the liberation struggle, and a reiteration that ZANU(PF) considered itself the custodian of national freedom.[12] Chenjerai Hunzvi weighed in: 'These whites are using stooges and puppets with the objective of taking over the government. It has happened in Eastern Europe where trade unions and human rights groups were used by foreign forces to destroy their own economies.'[13] And so, from the point of view of the government and its supporters, the charge was formed that Morgan Tsvangirai could be identified with urban labour, white farmers and foreign forces in a fight against socialism and the heritage of liberation. ZANU(PF) never departed from that early analysis and accusation.

The first assassination attempt against Tsvangirai came in December 1997 – so the first indication, the shot across the bows, of hard intimidation also came early. The ZCTU responded with three successful strikes in 1998 – in March and two in November – and there were further demonstrations and riots in May (although it is not clear whether the ZCTU had anything to do with these). It seemed in 1998 that there was everything to play for and that the government had no real sense of future strategy or of self-renewal.[14]

n early 1998 the National Constitutional Assembly (NCA) was med. It was a coalition of civic, human rights, and church groups, vyers, NGOs, and the ZCTU. Its basic initial intent was to campaign for constitutional reform. When, in April 1999, the government responded by establishing a constitutional commission, the NCA declined to participate in its work, accusing the new commission of being too controlled by President Mugabe. Because the work of the NCA was primarily to do with constitutional alternatives it propelled Tsvangirai into a political arena that was no longer solely concerned with economic matters. It is fair to say that, although Tsvangirai came of age in terms of economic matters with the *Beyond ESAP* document of 1996, and in terms of his capacities for national mobilisation with the December 1997 strike, it was his participation in the NCA from 1998 to 1999 that matured his understanding of constitutional and legal issues, and refined his sense of what good governance entailed. That good governance was manifestly fading in Zimbabwe could be seen from an increasing repressiveness on the part of the government. The first beatings of journalists took place in early 1999 amidst reports of army unrest. Even the idiosyncratic fellow-traveller with ZANU(PF), the editor of the *Mirror*, Ibbo Mandaza, had his features enhanced by being beaten in police cells.

It would be easy to draw a straight line to describe the upwards trajectory at this stage of Morgan Tsvangirai. Two things, however, should not be forgotten. The first is that he became more popular as the government became less so. Bombarding high-density suburbs with tear gas from helicopters as early as the January 1998 riots hardly endeared the government to the urban public. The second is that, with the economy already in serious difficulty, Robert Mugabe embarked in 1998 on a military campaign in the Congo and, by 1999, Zimbabwean soldiers were dying and the effort was costing the Zimbabwean exchequer £1 million per day. Moreover, it soon became clear that, while the military objectives of the Congo adventure were unclear, the opportunity for plunder on the part of senior officers and politicians was very clear. The opportunism and selfishness, built on the suffering and deaths of ordinary people, seemed to encapsulate an entire critique of what ZANU(PF) had become. The outgrowth from the NCA of the MDC as a political party owed as much to government misadventure as to the maturing of a sense of both principled and technocratic opposition. The new party was launched on 11 September 1999, and its first Congress was held on 30 January 2000. With Tsvangirai elected its president, and another senior ZCTU figure, Gibson Sibanda, its vice-president, it came into being with an urban trade union imprint which, despite the exposure to the NCA, it never entirely lost.

Tsvangirai, in his January acceptance speech, made three points. The first was that the MDC stood for an end to the internal plunder of Zimbabwe by a few. It stood for an end to plunder in the Congo. 'Zimbabwe has no strategic interest in the Congo.' And it stood for a rejection of the constitutional commission's proposed reforms at the national referendum the government had called for 12-13 February 2000.[15] But there was no mention in his speech of rural inequities, of land ownership or reform, or of any racial fault-lines in the old or projected new Zimbabwe.

Here again, with the referendum looming, it is important to make two points. The government was putting forward a series of constitutional reforms which were very much in its favour – but they had been publicly debated, so the move towards a more authoritarian constitutional state had been transparent. The government was entering the referendum in bullying good faith. It was sure it would win, and marginalise the new opposition party. The almost naive misreading of the situation would not be repeated by ZANU(PF) – but this, coupled with the momentum the MDC had generated with its launch, meant that for the first time there would be a defeat at the polls for ZANU(PF). This is not to say that ZANU(PF) fought cleanly. Far from it – but it fouled in a lackadaisical manner, as if it were the elite Dynamos football team about to crush a reserve Wankie side. Morgan Tsvangirai saw the opportunity opening up and campaigned alongside the National Constitutional Assembly with amazing energy.

The constitutional package put forward by ZANU(PF) would have given increased powers to President Mugabe. In that sense, the referendum was as close to a vote of confidence that Zimbabwe had ever had. It was also proposed to legitimate land nationalisation without compensation and, to that extent, the referendum was a test of the ZANU(PF) vision of how it would complete its nationalist project – albeit 20 years after independence as a nation had been won. The constitutional package was rejected by 697,754 votes to 578,210. Although this represented only 26 per cent of the electorate voting, the result was hailed as a triumph by the MDC – and indeed it was. ZANU(PF) was stunned, knew it had not taken sufficient steps to ensure its supporters voted, and realised that the MDC was not going to be another marginal opposition party, that Morgan Tsvangirai was not going to be another Edgar Tekere, who had challenged Mugabe in 1990, failed – albeit with violence clouding the campaign – and shrank from sight thereafter. Jonathan Moyo immediately announced what the new battle-lines would be:

> Preliminary figures show there were 100,000 white people voting. We have never seen anything like that in this country. They were all over town. Everyone who observed will tell you there were long queues of whites. The difference between the 'yes' and 'no' votes would not have been what it was had it not been for this vote.[16]

ıgabe had not used his new alliance with the war veterans in the ɛrendum campaign. It seemed now that ZANU(PF), having lost an electoral test for the first time, needed to field some shock troops. Two weeks after the referendum was lost, at the end of February, the war veterans began their invasions of white-owned farms. At a stroke, Mugabe and Hunzvi transformed the downturn of the economy into a precipitate slide, paved the way for hunger and malnutrition in Zimbabwe, and stole back the political ground on which all future contests would be fought. If ZANU(PF) had not foreseen the possibility of an MDC triumph, the MDC had not foreseen with what devastating effect the Mugabe/Hunzvi, ZANU(PF)/war veterans axis could move into position.

Elections & treason

Parliamentary elections were called for 24-25 June 2000. This was five months after the first MDC Party Congress, four months after the farm invasions began. By now the land issue had become a huge international cause for concern – but the British in particular seemed to concentrate on the plight of white farmers, and only secondarily protest against the increasingly brutal treatment being meted out to MDC supporters. The support for white farmers allowed Mugabe and ZANU(PF) to inject a rhetoric of accusation into the election campaign. They accused Britain of racism – white ownership rights over the historical rights of black people – and of unreformed imperialism in trying to tell Zimbabwe what it could or could not do. Tsvangirai was labelled a stooge of the British.

Simultaneously, the courts were being defied by Hunzvi, while ZANU(PF) set about plans for new legislation to give legality to the land seizures; and to change the composition of the courts. Political crackdown was to affect not only the MDC. But it was the street violence and rural violence that most affected the MDC campaigners. By the end of the first week of June, 1,400 farms had been occupied but 29 MDC workers had been killed, 14 in April alone. In April Tsvangirai was saying, 'we are not throwing in the towel. Our people are being killed but we will continue.'[17] By May, MDC cadres were opening their rallies by singing a song: 'Mother and Father, if I die today don't cry for me. It is I who gave myself to die for Zimbabwe.'[18] By this time the MDC was organising itself by the hectic use of mobile phones. Denied sufficient terrestrial lines, and anxious about eavesdropping, all campaign organisation was accomplished by these phones – mobiles being then a relatively new phenomenon in Zimbabwe, new enough for the government not yet to have eavesdropping equipment able to be used against them. Mobiles and their numbers were interchanged constantly among leading cadres. If the government did learn to eavesdrop it would never be certain who had which phone (the MDC sometimes lost track as well). The campaign was, in short, chaotic and extremely courageous.

But, on the government side, preparations for the election were also proceeding. The intimidation of MDC workers and potential supporters was clearly orchestrated centrally. The ZANU(PF) campaign, with its theme of nationalism and its accusations of British neo-imperialism, was unremitting. With all of this, however, the actual days of polling were relatively quiet and, although there were clear cases of local abuses – which the MDC were, often successfully, to challenge in the courts – there seemed no evidence of co-ordinated national rigging. The MDC was still very young and the economic decline of Zimbabwe had not yet reached catastrophic proportions. The ZANU(PF) heartland was prepared, at this stage, to hold its nerve. Even so, the MDC ran ZANU(PF) very close indeed. The government took 62 seats, the opposition 58 (57 MDC; 1 ZANU-Ndonga, the minority party of Ndabaningi Sithole). Later court and by-election victories would, for a short time, equalise the elected parliamentary seats between government and opposition, and ZANU(PF) would have to depend upon the 30 MPs appointed without election by the President. By-election defeats for the MDC much later in the parliamentary term would see a shift back to ZANU(PF) but, at the 2000 elections, ZANU(PF) lost all nineteen seats in Harare and all eight seats in Bulawayo. Of the fifiteen remaining seats in Matabeleland, the MDC won thirteen. In short, the great cities fell to the MDC, as did most of Matabeleland – mindful of what a ZANU(PF) government had done in launching the Fifth Brigade to terrorise and murder so many citizens there in the 1980s. Very little of the remaining country-side was captured by the MDC. The presence of war veterans, and the lack of a true MDC rural policy, not to mention a sustained rural campaign (and such campaign as there was had been intimidatory), meant that the urban bias of the MDC's foundation was reflected in the urban victories it achieved, but it also demonstrated its weakness in the traditional ZANU(PF) strongholds.

After the parliamentary elections there was, for much of the remainder of 2000, an uneasy stand-off between the MDC and ZANU(PF) – both now getting used to a more complex political landscape, and the MDC parliamentarians learning how to operate as MPs. The government continued its land seizures, however, and began preparing its turnover of court judges, and introducing broad bands of new legislation – both sanctioning 'fast track' land redistribution and clamping down on the press. The MDC opposed all these measures, but it must be said that by far the most resonant intervention was made by a ZANU(PF) stalwart, Edison Zvobgo. It was he who, in September 2000, attacked Mugabe over the land issue with the now famous rds: 'We have tainted what was a glorious revolution, reducing it to ne agrarian racist enterprise.'

But if it was Zvobgo who was stingingly eloquent it was Tsvangirai who proved to be clumsy. In October 2000, after having watched on television the Belgrade crowds peacefully occupy parliament and depose the Yugoslav President Milosevic, he predicted that the fate of Mugabe – if he did not voluntarily step aside – would prove to be similar. The government immediately laid charges of incitement to violence and later, almost as a signal of a more serious effort to come, added a charge of treason. At that stage, the charge of treason was for rhetorical effect, but it meant that Mugabe now considered that the gloves were off. He was certainly not going to allow a crowd of MDC supporters to march into State House, peacefully or not. Thereafter, every MDC show of force – demonstrations, boycotts and stayaways – was met by resolute and increasingly brutal police action. The centre of Harare could resemble a ring of steel, and tear gas would hover for hours over flashpoints of unrest. Protesters would be savagely beaten, even when they took refuge in their own homes, and deaths occurred. In July 2001, eleven people were killed, 61 disappeared, and 288 were tortured in the escalating violence.[19] It was clear by July 2001 that the opposition had run out of ideas. All its urban strength could be thrown against Mugabe and come to nothing. And yet it had no alternative strategy and never devised one. It was about this time that the infamous video was recorded of Tsvangirai in discussion with Ari Ben-Manashe, talking about the elimination of Mugabe.

Almost as if scripted, the video was released in an Australian television documentary on 13 February 2002, shortly before the delayed Commonwealth summit in Brisbane (it had been delayed from October 2001 because of terrorist fears after 9/11). The summit was in turn a week before the Presidential elections in Zimbabwe, 9-10 March 2002. Tsvangirai was charged with treason, along with other senior MDC figures, on 25 February. From the ZANU(PF) perspective, the timing was perfect – not just for local consumption but as international evidence that it was not only Mugabe who could be charged with anti-democratic tendencies. Whether it was entrapment of Tsvangirai or not, the British immediately walked into the trap, rushing to defend Tsvangirai without having actually first seen the video.

The remainder of the story to date is well-known. Amidst intimidation, great delays at the polls, and almost-certain rigging, Robert Mugabe defeated Morgan Tsvangirai's Presidential challenge 1,685,212 votes to 1,258,401. In the years since then inflation has soared continuously; the printing of banknotes has not kept up with the constant need for high denominations – and even with banknotes, petrol and other modern necessities have been in critical shortage; malnutrition has stalked the countryside; the bulk of the seized land is not being farmed and much of it has not in any case been given to the poor; the only truly independent daily newspaper has been forced into closure; Zimbabwe has left the Commonwealth and is unable to send significant numbers of its ministerial and ruling elites to Europe and the US because of sanctions; and Tsvangirai, also unable to travel abroad because of his bail conditions, has watched the nation of Zimbabwe unravelling even as ZANU(PF) keeps emphasising its project of nationalism. Tsvangirai has kept up the fight. He has campaigned unremittingly and despite constant harassment. The axe attack in early July 2004 was only the latest in a long line of actions against both the MDC and himself. The MDC has begun losing by-elections and there are factions within the MDC eyeing the leadership – but Tsvangirai has never stopped. The treason verdict, at time of writing, had not yet been pronounced.

In many ways, the end of July was a bleak time to interview Morgan Tsvangirai. It had been a very tough winter in more than one respect. But, to an external observer, there had been one curiosity about the entire Zimbabwean episode from 2000 to the present day. It is Morgan Tsvangirai who is leader of the opposition. Yet it is the President who talks as if he were the one who was in opposition. Curiously, he sounds like Tony Blair before he became Prime Minister – attacking the ruling party – confrontational, scathing, taking no prisoners, scoring points and predicting his opponent's downfall. At no time in his career has he seemed less Presidential. Tsvangirai's speech has had a very different flavour, and it seemed that this would be an ideal entry point for our long conversations.

Notes

1. Bloomington: Indiana University Press, 2003.
2. Curiously, the full-length analysis of those 1990 elections was written by Jonathan Moyo. The early stages of the project saw the involvement of John Makumbe, now a noted civic society campaigner, and Welshman Ncube, now a senior figure within the MDC and thought to be the leader of its intellectual faction. It is an ironic rather than point-scoring note that I wish to strike in quoting from Moyo's Acknowledgements: 'Anyone familiar with politics in Zimbabwe... would readily be aware of the potential hazards of electoral research. The risks are real, numerous and sometimes very dangerous.... During the fieldwork some of the students were detained by over-zealous personnel from the Central Intelligence Organisation and some elements in the army and police who were prone to manipulation by the ruling ZANU(PF) party, basically because they did not understand their constitutional duties.' Jonathan N. Moyo, *Voting for Democracy: Electoral Politics in Zimbabwe*, Harare: University of Zimbabwe Publications, 1992.
3. Cited in Richard Saunders, 'Life in Space – the New Politics of Zimbabwe', *southern African Review of Books*, 5:1, 1993, p. 19. This was also a pointed dig at Ibbo Mandaza, publisher of the *Southern African Political and Economic Monthly*

(even though the original Tsvangirai article appeared in exactly that journal), which was published from Mandaza's 'mansion' in Deary Avenue, opposite the Royal Harare Golf Club – although it was no more or less a mansion than the house in which Tsvangirai now lives.

4. For my account of the 1991 Zambian elections, and a comparison with the 1990 elections in Zimbabwe, see Stephen Chan, 'Democracy in southern Africa: the 1990 Elections in Zimbabwe and 1991 Elections in Zambia', *The Round Table*, Issue 322, 1992, although Robert Mugabe may now be more interested in Chiluba's fate after Chiluba's own departure from power and subsequent arraignment on charges of corruption. For thorough accounts of the entire Zambian electoral experience from 1991 to Chiluba's departure in 2001, see the two special double issues of *African Social Research*, Nos 45 and 46 (misnumbered on the cover as 55 and 56) 2001, and Nos 47 and 48, 2002.

5. Brian Raftopoulos, 'Nationalism and Labour in Salisbury, 1953–1965', in Brian Raftopoulos and Tsuneo Yoshikuni (eds), *Sites of Struggle: Essays in Zimbabwe's Urban History*, Harare: Weaver Press, 1999.

6. Lloyd Sachikonye, 'Trade Unions, Economic and Political Development in Zimbabwe since Independence', in Brian Raftopoulos and Ian Phimister (eds), *Keep On Knocking: A History of the Labour Movement in Zimbabwe 1900-97*, Harare: Baobab Books, 1997.

7. See Yash Tandon, 'Trade Unions and Labour in the Agricultural Sector in Zimbabwe', in Brian Raftopoulos & Lloyd Sachikonye (eds), *Striking Back: The Labour Movement and the Post-Colonial State in Zimbabwe 1980-2000*, Harare: Weaver Press, 2001.

8. Jeffrey Herbst, *State Politics in Zimbabwe*, Berkeley: University of California Press, 1990, pp. 219, 255.

9. Brian Raftopoulos, 'The Labour Movement and the Emergence of Opposition Politics in Zimbabwe', in Raftopoulos and Sachikonye (eds), op. cit., p. 10. It should be pointed out that what is encompassed in the above quotes is a range of debate involving scholars such as Paris Yeros, Patrick Bond, Edward Webster and Glen Adler. Raftopoulos gives full credit, and citations, to these people. My depiction here does take summary to a new extreme.

10. Ibid., p. 12. Raftopoulos cites his interview with Tsvangirai a year after the meeting with Hunzvi as his source.

11. *Financial Gazette* (Harare), 11 December 1997.

12. *The Sunday Herald* (Harare), 22 February 1998.

13. *The Herald* (Harare), 5 March 1998.

14. It seemed at the time that the government had definitely run out of ideas. For my assessment of the first part of 1998, see Stephen Chan, 'Troubled Pluralisms: Pondering an Indonesian Moment for Zimbabwe and Zambia', *The Round Table*, Issue 349, 1999.

15. *The Guardian* (London), 31 January 2000.

16. *The Times* (London), 16 February 2000.

17. *The Observer* (London), 30 April 2000.

18. *The Independent on Sunday* (London), 21 May 2000.

19. *The Guardian* (London), 20 August 2001.

Inclusiveness & Opposition

One of the products of Westminster democracy is the idea of an opposition party. It is able to contest elections and perhaps become the government. Meantime, its duty – not just its right – is to oppose the current elected government. It does this not necessarily because its policies are more correct than those of the government but because its constitutional position is as an important check and balance to government power. This works best when there is a united, or not too seriously disunited, opposition. Britain and the US, with two powerful parties, provide the best examples of the idea at work.

Because it has indeed worked as an important obstacle to authoritarian government, the British, in the decolonisation period, sought to export this style of democracy to its former colonies. It was also encouraged to do so since Britain had recently spent long years in a war against totalitarian dictatorship and was then also involved in a struggle against what it saw as totalitarian Communist rule. Democracy was the international alternative to the lack of political freedom in the Eastern bloc, and political independence and political freedom were thought to go hand in hand. After the fall of Communism in 1989, the West sought to encourage multiparty democracies in the Eastern European countries. There have always been difficulties with the model in its new locations. In Eastern Europe the springing into life of often dozens of political parties meant little coalescence in opposition to the government. Moreover, the concept of opposition was not that of a loyal duty but borrowed instead from the idea of being opposed to authoritarian rule. The style was one of resistance and not of checks and balances. In Africa, postcolonial leaders such as Nyerere and Kaunda complained that opposition parties allowed the electorate to be divided along ethnic lines, and ethnic divisions would ruin the young nationalist projects in their countries. The African one-party state, which was a commonplace throughout the 1970s to the early 1990s, was a response to this. And, in Asian states such as Singapore, the more subtle device emerged of the dominant-party state. Opposition parties were allowed, but constrained; dissent was allowed, but within limits. To all intents and purposes, the opposition became a decoration, something that legitimised the democratic claims of Singapore while being itself evidence that democracy had very clear limits. Only in India, and there with trauma and violence, and in the face of manipulation and illiteracy, has a Westminster-style democracy triumphed in the face of all odds.

What is happening in Zimbabwe is a lurch towards a dominant-party state – only with considerably greater violence and crudity than in Singapore. It comes at the time when the rest of Africa is labouring – often successfully – towards more genuinely balanced multiparty democracies. Unlike the Singaporean model, however, which is based on economic success and the government's role in ensuring that success, the Zimbabwean model is based on a liberation history – those who won liberation also won the right to develop nationalism – and economic well-being is not a first-order justification. It is important to note that the right claimed is to develop nationalism – not just the nation, but the sort of national consciousness that holds the nation together. This goes beyond Singapore, as it claims a right over public thought and not just public action.

This is to put matters in a very broad perspective. There are senior members of ZANU(PF) who are horrified at such a direction and hope it will be temporary – but, guardedly, see it being modified only when the MDC accepts its place as a subsidiary aspect of Zimbabwean politics. And, in the curious meeting of minds that can characterise even Zimbabwean politics, some senior members of the MDC feel that their party has overplayed its hand. This might account for some of the much-rumoured faction-fighting within the MDC.

Even so, the broad approach of ZANU(PF) and its mode of recent government has been to act aggressively. A liberation force fights against someone else who claims legitimacy. In the case of the MDC, its claims of moral legitimacy and its charge that ZANU(PF) has forfeited democratic legitimacy by its rigging of elections and violence towards citizens are particularly galling to a government party that views itself as historically legitimate. The assault against the MDC is not only so that ZANU(PF) can retain power but so that ZANU(PF) can continue to inherit the mantle of legitimacy on its own terms. ZANU(PF) is against the legitimacy of an opposition that has grown too large. The ZANU(PF) response has not been to govern better, but to attack harder.

In a way ZANU(PF) has no option. Far from having provided the economic success of Singapore it has presided over the most precipitate economic slide in modern African history. The most recent collapse has happened in two phases, the first from 1997 to 2000 occasioned by the sudden capitulation to the war veterans and participation in the war in the Congo; the second from 2000 initiated by the land invasions and the consequent reduction of agricultural productivity, and the climate of violence with its subsequent loss of investment revenue. The MDC has attacked these things. Morgan Tsvangirai has attacked Mugabe, and the likening of his fate to Milosevic's was indeed an implicit threat – if not necessarily a direct one. By that time it was clear in any case that the MDC days of action had no chance of storming parliament. But, having said that, the discourse of the MDC has been more inclusive than that of ZANU(PF). Government ministers thunder at the opposition. President Mugabe says he will bury the opposition at the March 2005 elections. The rhetoric remains consistently aggressive – as if ZANU(PF) were resisting the MDC. As if, in an East European version of Westminster, it were itself the opposition party resisting the one with established electoral legitimacy. There is something inverted about Zimbabwean politics that all the ruling triumphalism cannot disguise. Moreover, even in the heavily suspect electoral victory of 2002, it was not President Mugabe who gracefully published his thanks to his followers. Tsvangirai's statement towards the end of polling is worth reprinting in full:

> My Fellow Zimbabweans: I thank you for your courage as you continue to vote in your millions. We see your determination. We hear your support. We share your impatience. The power is in your hands. What the people of Zimbabwe now deserve is a celebration.
>
> But there are those who say that dark clouds threaten the horizon of our country.
>
> Together we have travelled a very difficult road to achieve democratic change. Your resilience to reclaim your rights, as expressed by the overwhelming turnout, has shaken the corridors of power. Rarely in the history of mankind have a people faced such brutality while retaining such gracious exuberance.
>
> But the forces of darkness may yet try to block your path to victory.
>
> As I address you, it is sad that this regime still seems intent on defying your will. Whatever may happen, I as your loyal servant am with you all the way. They may want to arrest me and at worst kill me, but they will never destroy the spirit of the people to reclaim their power. We may have moments of fear but we must never let despair overwhelm us.
>
> The tide of change is irreversible but we must be prepared to pay a high price for our freedom. President Mugabe and his colleagues are afraid of the people and we have heard they may do anything to kill the messenger. If they do, you must stay strong and carry on the work we began together. Among you walk heroes – heroes who waited hours and hours to vote, heroes who refused to be turned away. These are the heroes of the new Zimbabwe whose voices must be heard around the world.
>
> Now is the time we have been waiting for and we are ready. But let us first wait peacefully for your votes to be cast and counted. Restrain yourselves so you do not allow their sinister plans to succeed. As you wait for the results, do not succumb to their provocative traps. I know they are trying very hard to provoke you. Yes, we share your fear that the result will be rigged, but let us complete the process we began together in our campaign for a better life for

ll Zimbabweans.

In closing, let us pray President Mugabe, his party and the security forces shall uphold the Constitution while peacefully honouring and respecting the will of the Zimbabwean people.

May the Lord bless you in your continued efforts for freedom.[1]

In this single statement, the words 'we', 'us', and 'our' – words of inclusion – are used 17 times. Patience and non-violence are urged and, despite the low-key charges of possible rigging and definite provocation, President Mugabe is urged only to respect the Constitution. No retribution is promised him. Tsvangirai describes himself as a 'servant' and as someone willing to be killed for the common cause. Perhaps a foreboding of death began at that time, helping to explain the calm that he exuded during our conversations: living with it and expecting its possibility somehow defuses its threat. In that case the government effort to intimidate Tsvangirai has had precisely the opposite effect. And he seeks in the text above to recast the meaning of heroism. It is not a title reserved for those who fought for liberation, but also for those who patiently and peacefully fought for democracy. The MDC has not been free from its own use of violence, but it has been a minor feature of its campaigns and pales beside the full-throttled violence often used against it. Insofar as anything in Africa has come close to a Gandhian campaign, the MDC effort is it, and non-violence was also a hallmark of this single but comprehensive statement of basic principle in the face of adversity.

In the early 1990s, when Tsvangirai was still leading the trade union movement, the linguist Alison Love studied the way he constructed his speech and compared it with that of a ZANU(PF) minister – both of them addressing the same conference on structural adjustment and political democracy.[2] Whereas the minister's speech was declaratory and assertive, expressing its points as self-evident, uninviting of interaction, and seeking to depict government action as both natural and for the national benefit – a reflection of its sense of long-term hegemony – Tsvangirai's speech used a range of 'linguistic resources' to present alternatives to the minister's points. He seldom disagreed outright with the minister but introduced a number of qualifying and conditional clauses. 'We accept that it [structural adjustment] will succeed, but it will succeed in making a few people richer and the majority of people poor.' He pointed out difficulties in fulfilling the minister's predictions for improved economic output but, again, did not dismiss them outright. He raised questions and posed the need for alternatives. Tsvangirai's speech can be seen as an attempt to transform the discursive event of the seminar from a reception of top-down government policy statement to an interactive critique of policy and a formulation of alternatives. He 'problematised' what the minister said. This is considerably different from rejecting it. Alison Love concluded that such speech was a precondition to a proper democratic discourse, and its interactivity – its inclusiveness in the asking of questions and suggesting searches for alternatives – made the speech far from 'crudely oppositional'. Being inclusive and not 'crudely oppositional' is a hard act to pull off, so I began our conversations by asking Tsvangirai about this.

I think you must understand here my background. I think it's very important to dwell on that. My upbringing. Frustrations of my young years. Lack of opportunity. Then, later on, my representative capacity for the urban workers. And I think the other defining character is the fact that struggle is itself inclusive. The struggle against colonialism was very inclusive, it cut across the traditional divisions of class, of gender and position – for the blacks I must say. And this current struggle cuts across again in a similar vein. Freedom is something cherished across colour, across class, gender, status. The moment we came out of the labour movement to form this broad movement, it had to be inclusive in character.

I think we are all... I think society is at a stage where it's in a transitional phase. Everyone realises that society is in transition and everyone is preoccupied with how to achieve this change. There are dominant forces. The labour movement has been a dominant force and because of its dominance it has been able to attract other diverse groups to the struggle. But how do we keep all this together? Sometimes it surprises me also. But I suppose the main focus and the main objective, the goal, of this whole broad democratic movement is to cross the hurdle of transition from the nationalist phase to a more democratic phase.

I said we would come later to a deeper look at nationalism and its discontents. I didn't want to lose the thread of inclusiveness at this stage. I remarked that I had not come across any article of the sort Alison Love had written about any other contemporary African leader. It was at this point that Tsvangirai began sensing that this was not going to be yet another interview, another journalist seeking a sound bite or at best a short series of sound bites. We were not going to jump about from topic to topic to amass an anthology of short quotes. He looked hard at me from across the desk, looked through me to the lawn being watered outside, and began.

Look... yes... I suppose that you set yourself a particular vision. You define a certain path to achieve that vision... and I have been literally preoccupied in my conscious and my subconscious way about how we have been betrayed. It's almost as if... as if we thought 'it can't happen to us'. You know the feeling. And yet for the past twenty years it has been like we have been betrayed. I remember in 1988, when I joined the ZCTU, I had already been in the labour movement. And I think it was shortly after then, the greatest betrayal was my first arrest. My experience over my first arrest, and the reasons given, really shook my confidence in Mugabe.³ I would have forgiven him before that, but after that I realised that the man I had held in very high esteem could actually turn out to be the antithesis, the real opposite of what I believed the whole struggle was all about.

It should be said that although Tsvangirai was indeed treated very roughly and had to spend six weeks in detention in 1989 this was not in itself a great moment in the ZCTU history. Rather, it was a moment for civil society as a whole – deeply disturbed by the revelations and first repercussions of the Willowgate scandal involving the corrupt purchase of Mazda cars. This was small-time corruption compared with what was to come, but it was a shock to a society that had come to pride itself that it was somehow different, perhaps immune to the 'disease of Africa'. The students were at the forefront of this disquiet, and the ZCTU came in to support the students. Moreover, other actors in both the region and Zimbabwe itself were attracting more attention than Tsvangirai. In August 1989, the new South African President de Klerk was visiting neighbouring Zambia, right on the Victoria Falls border with Zimbabwe, to explore the first steps towards the ending of apartheid; and, in Zimbabwe itself, it was Edgar Tekere as leader of the young Zimbabwe Unity Movement (ZUM) who was gearing up for the first national electoral challenge to Mugabe in 1990 – and encountering a huge range of harassments. As much as complaining about corruption, the students were supporting Tekere. I was in Zimbabwe at the time and tried to witness the closing down of the university. By the time I got there, armed security was everywhere. The student leaders too had been arrested. Afterwards, the Vice-Chancellor showed me the new padded and barred doors he had had installed to prevent future stormings of his office – whether by students or security forces wasn't clear – but that first university closure of the post-independence era made 1989 a year of symbols that closed the first decade of independence. Harare was rife with rumours of behind-the-scenes political manoeuvres and even the most idealistic member of ZANU(PF) knew that the era of innocence (if you could have innocently ignored what had happened in Matabeleland) was over.⁴ Tsvangirai therefore was reflecting not just on his own experience, which was bitter enough, but on a much more widespread and popular emergence from blind faith in Mugabe. I put it to him that if he, Tsvangirai, and the MDC were seeking inclusiveness, an era of ZANU(PF) exclusiveness – of excluding others – dated from 1989. But Tsvangirai dated it from earlier in the post-independence era.

I think the patronage system Mugabe had put in place was already exclusive. You were either 'one of us' or not 'one of us'. You were either inside ZANU(PF) or outside it. If you were outside you were just excluded. For me you can't just put that date [1989] on it. I remember in the early years the way they tried to exclude Joshua Nkomo from having liberation credentials, from the legacy of the struggle, deliberately trying to exclude him, just because he was not in ZANU(PF) and was seen as an enemy. And, later on, this was manifest with the trade union movement. The moment the trade union movement tried to define its autonomy, outside the control of ZANU(PF), it became excluded from national projects, from government confidence, it became something labelled as alien to the liberation struggle. There were even accusations that the labour movement was never part of – did not take part in – the liberation struggle. Which I find ridiculous. Because, you know, the whole essence of the nationalist struggle, the birth of the nationalist struggle, came out of the labour movement. So I found this exclusion quite hurting. So, if you want to put a date, I can't, because I think it's an ongoing systematic exclusion.

Even as our conversation was beginning to move freely, there was still evidence that Tsvangirai was choosing his words carefully. The term 'essence of the nationalist struggle' and the statement that this essence originated with the labour movement is arguably true. The first recorded strike by black workers took place, involving miners, in 1895, a year ahead of the first chimurenga.[5] In the early 20th century there were three black miners' strikes before World War I. In 1919 there were strikes by miners, railway workers and municipal workers. To be fair, there were also strikes by white miners at the time, and the only really organised union was white. Although the Industrial and Commercial Workers' Union was established with black membership and grew in the 1920s, it remains fair to say that such avenues of resistance as there were in the early part of the century included not only the organisation of labour but cultural groups such as burial and dance societies,[6] and the Watch Tower movement – now more commonly known as Jehovah's Witnesses – with its fierce doctrine of equality before God's judgement.[7] It wasn't really until the end of World War II and the formation of railway and other unions that black labour could be said to have become organised. In April 1948 there was a general strike involving 100,000 black workers. Legislation in 1950, the Subversive Activities Act, was intended to control the political agenda of the unions; and it was in 1951 that the two parts of Tsvangirai's statement coalesced, with Joshua Nkomo becoming the first full-time General Secretary of the Rhodesian Railways African Employees' Association. In 1956, the entire leadership of what was now the Railway African Workers' Union was arrested. In 1957 the new African National Congress was formed with Nkomo as head. It was banned in 1959, with 300 detained. It was succeeded in 1960 by the National Democratic Party, with Nkomo as head from October that year. Thereafter, Robert Mugabe became an office-holder in the NDC. By 1964, competition between Nkomo and Mugabe had become intense. It has to be said that from the Unilateral Declaration of Independence in 1965, till official independence in 1980, the labour movement was no longer a major player in the nationalist struggle now taken up by Nkomo and Mugabe's separate political parties. But Tsvangirai is correct to talk of an historical essence, and also to link that with Nkomo. ZANU(PF) has not gone out of its way to celebrate the industrial and labour origins of nationalism, and its treatment of Nkomo is well known. Tsvangirai is not correct to infer a labour foundation for nationalism after 1965, but he is certainly correct in talking about the excluding tendency of ZANU(PF). I asked him about the formidable ZANU(PF) internal party discipline which, even if it excludes others, makes it so hard for those within – even if they are plotting factions – to escape inclusion. How can the MDC fight such discipline that so fiercely includes and regulates its own while excluding all others?

> *Well, I'm sure one would have to say that any force has a counter-force. The more that formidable force alienates itself from the people, the more a counter-force will be built outside it. And the weaker the pillars of support for that force will become. Doubt will grow. I mean internal doubt within ZANU(PF). I was a member of ZANU(PF). There was a stage when I started building my own internal doubt about the credibility of ZANU(PF). This is the betrayal I was talking about. So it reached a stage when I said 'no'. I think the people have to find alternative formations. We have to create the alternative movement of the people, because the crisis we were facing is a result of this betrayal. An alternative was possible because of the weaknesses and the betrayal within ZANU(PF).*

I replied that, nevertheless, ZANU(PF) was at the present time attempting its own forms of greater outreach and inclusiveness. Some of these are cruder than others, but some are quite subtle. In the wake of Oliver Mtukudzi's 2000 'Bvuma' album, with its lyrics that seemed to suggest Mugabe should stand down – something sung knowingly all over the nation – ZANU(PF) had been composing its own songs and jingles that can be insidiously catchy. Children sing them in the high-density suburbs, and the rumour is that Jonathan Moyo himself composes them.

> *Well, we have no experience of doing this. But we do see this attempt by ZANU(PF) to be inclusive. The war veterans were brought in. We know that now, after that, after having first excluded the chiefs,*

28

they are now bringing the chiefs and traditional rulers back in. Yes, it is an effort at inclusiveness, but you know ZANU(PF) has a self-contradictory pattern. If they say, 'you must be one of us', it means others will be excluded. Now they are trying to include the unlawful operators, the militias, the youth militias, they are trying to bring them on. It's because as we move on, as we encompass more, ZANU(PF) must have realised that its own pillars of support are very thin, they stand on a thin base. So they needed to rally their people behind patriotic credentials, its liberation credentials and its liberation legacy. The difficulty here is that the economic and social conditions do not favour their patronage. They cannot extend patronage to the young unemployed, to trade union demands, to business demands. They cannot extend patronage over and over again because of the thin economic base.

I reiterated the role of Jonathan Moyo, mentioning the intellectual and nationalist foundation for his strategy: an inclusiveness certainly because of also excluding. A strategy that says it includes all blacks in a continuing black revolution, an antithesis of earlier white domination and it of course tends to be excluding of all whites.

Well, it's a rallying cry. I noticed, immediately after the [2000] referendum, I think it dawned on Mugabe and others that they had lost the support of the people and, obviously, they had to find a rallying point – especially one that concerned the grievances that predominate within the black population. One is the racism of the whites. One can easily say, 'you see, the reason why we have problems is because of these white racists.' Two, one can refer to the past colonial attitudes of white regimes in this country. And, three, pan-African solidarity. It's a good agenda for rallying a black population. The grievances of land, issues of economic inequality, of poverty, are all more easily sold because the population wants to have justified why it is that it is being deprived, why all these problems when independence is supposed to have created a better life for all. As if independence hadn't actually come. For people wanted to believe Mugabe. They did believe Mugabe. They believed in the liberation struggle. They believed in the new society coming out of liberation. They kept on hopelessly hoping that, one day, things would turn around, and all they have seen is the opposite.

What had been emerging from our discussions was certainly the sense that Tsvangirai was committed to inclusiveness and opposed to exclusiveness, but that he also saw his own experience under arrest and detention in 1989 as personifying the excluding nature of ZANU(PF). He had felt personally betrayed, and saw the nation in turn as a nation in the process of being betrayed. But, could we get behind what Tsvanirai called the 'liberation credentials' and 'patriotic credentials' of ZANU(PF)'s self-justification, and discuss what Terence Ranger had called the very ownership of 'patriotic history' – the idea that owning the past confers an ownership of the future, not because the past may be interpreted in any specific way, but that the interpretation itself may be owned, and that it may be owned because there is a process of seizing that ownership from a previously all-powerful white intellectual ownership of interpretation and of philosophy? Could the Tsvangirai who could talk in personal terms talk in another way?

Notes

1. MDC press release, 'Election Message from MDC President Morgan Tsvangirai', Harare, 11 March 2002.

2. Alison Love, 'Democratic Discourse? Realising alternatives in Zimbabwean political discourse', in *Zambezia: The Journal of Humanities of the University of Zimbabwe*, 27:1, 2000.

3. This was in October to November 1989, when University of Zimbabwe students protested against corruption. Tsvangirai expressed solidarity with the students and was arrested. Lloyd Sachikonye, 'Trade Unions: Economic and Political Development in Zimbabwe since Independence in 1980', in Brian Raftopoulos and Ian Phimister (eds), *Keep on Knocking: A History of the Labour Movement in Zimbabwe 1900–97*, Harare: Baobab Books, 1997, p. 119.

4. I wrote a satire on this after my 1989 visit. See Stephen Chan, 'Presidentialism in Lusaka and Harare', in *Wasafiri*, No. 12, 1990.

5. *Chimurenga* is a Shona word meaning to fight or struggle. The liberation struggle waged against the white settler state of Rhodesia in the 1970s was the second chimurenga. The more recent struggle to wrest the land back into the hands of 'the people' is sometimes referred to, in an effort to give it a liberation struggle mask, as the third chimurenga.

6. Despite the incredibly stilted language, on burial societies see Louis Masuko, 'The Zimbabwean Burial Societies', in Mahmood Mamdani and Ernest Wambia-dia-Wamba (eds), *African Studies in Social Movements and Democracy*, Dakar: CODESRIA, 1995. Some of these burial societies also took on elements of dance societies where resistance could be artistically inflected. See T.O. Ranger, *Dance and Society in Eastern Africa*, London: Heinemann, 1975, pp. 136-7.

7. Ian Phimister and Charles van Onselen, 'The Labour Movement in Zimbabwe 1900-1945', in Raftopoulos and Phimister, op. cit., pp. 10-12; Gerald Horne, *From the Barrel of a Gun*, Chapel Hill: University of North Carolina Press, 2001, p. 97. The most thorough study remains unpublished: Sholto Cross, 'The Watch Tower Movement in South Central Africa, 1908-1945', University of Oxford PhD thesis, 1973.

The Battle for Ownership of the Mind

Ali Mazrui, the Kenyan scholar who has spent most of his academic career at Makerere University in Uganda and then in US universities, wrote a book that, eleven years before 9/11, sought to introduce the idea that culture and cultural traditions had a major role to play in modern politics and that they could not be wished away.[1] He gave seven major functions of culture. The first is as a lens of perception. It conditions how we see the world. The second is the provision of a motivation for behaviour. It will make us respond to the same conditions in different ways according to our cultural backgrounds. The third is the provision of criteria for evaluation. What is regarded as beautiful or repugnant will differ from culture to culture. The fourth is the provision of a basis for identity. Rival forms of ethnic identity have led to genocide, have led to institutions such as apartheid. The fifth is the provision of a mode of communication. Different languages, originating from different cultures, will not always communicate exactly the same idea about what seems to be the same phenomenon. 'Lost in translation' is more than just a silly expression. The sixth is that it provides a basis for stratification. Class and rank, the foundations of class and rank, can determine priority in the allocation of high offices or scarce resources. The seventh lies in the system of production and consumption. This is not the basic Marxian precept that each should produce with equal labour, according to ability, so that each might equally consume, according to need. Rather it is to say that patterns of consumption can determine production. This last function of culture has multinational consequences. The need to consume much by certain people in country X might lead to the production of power relationships that ensure that economic assistance from country Y is consumed only by those people.

Mazrui went on to say that, in the US, many Black Studies courses and Afro-American Studies courses had cultural ambitions, i.e. they sought to recast the black person in terms of cultural functions that were no longer white American. In this, such courses had much in common with the négritude movement of Leopold Senghor and Aimé

Césaire in the Paris of the 1930s, when they sought to propose a black cultural distinctiveness that was both valuable and beautiful in its own right, but not determined by Western criteria.[2] Some of these ambitions are very evident in the academic texts studied on such courses. Work by Molefi Kete Asante and his disciple, Marimba Ba, is central here.[3] The problem is that the latter book is an amazing mélange of references to many different sorts of Europeanness and many different sorts of Africanness, as if two vast continents and all the cultures – plural – within them could be generalised, so that what is Malian is by extension also Zimbabwean, and what is Scandinavian is by extension also Greek. Even if this sort of generalising project could be accomplished there are four key problems.

The first is precisely one of essentialism. A culture becomes confined to what sets it apart from others. It becomes a protected preserve and, as a result, often cannot grow and absorb external influences – even beneficial ones. There are developing 'schools' of African philosophy – more correctly groups of like-minded philosophers – who wish to see an essentialism be given room to explore itself. However, as Barry Hallen has pointed out, there are contending schools or groups who recognise that all thought has already been cross-fertilised with the thought of others, and the task of separation is impossible.[4] An African socialism, of the sort Nyerere attempted, is still a crossover between European models and what were taken to be African ones – not to mention the admixture of state-led social-engineering. What, in any case, is a 'state', or even a 'nation', except that which responds to a modern Western series of typologies and definitions? A 'nationalist' project is, from the outset, inflected by external discourses.

The second is that a cultural project is not easily an economic one – especially in an era of globalised economics. An African culture can no sooner operate outside the global economy, and the politics of that economy, than a Japanese culture. As with the first problem the trick lies in getting the mixture right – but then the declarations of 'purity' can no longer be made. It is not possible to defy the economics of the world in the name of indigenous cultural values and expect to survive.

The third problem is that it is precisely the manipulation of culture and the cultural functions that Mazrui mentioned that has given rise to dictatorships. The Cameroonian scholar, Achille Mbembe, now working at Witwatersrand University, warned of what dictatorial state power seeks to do. It:

1. Politically creates its own world of meanings, which it aims to make so central that it aspires to affect all other worlds of meaning that exist in society.

2. Makes every effort to institutionalise its world of meanings as the 'social-historical world', in other words to turn it into reality by instilling it not only into the consciousness of its subjects or targets, but also into the world-view of the period.[5]

Mbembe also warned that successful dictatorships use the totality of the 'social-historical world', as defined by themselves or their parties, as a cover for their own corruption. Anyone who accuses them is against the cultural world and its values that the 'nation' has been led, or forced, to cherish; and under this cover they indulge in 'folly, pleasure and drunkeness'.[6]

And the fourth problem of any cultural or national essentialism, if it is African, is that – precisely because of historical and contemporary global cross-fertilisation, and because the research to uncover what is truly 'African' in terms of rigorous and codified linguistic and philosophical study is so young and underdeveloped – African knowledge is not yet truly available. Even an African scholar often regarded as an essentialist, V.Y. Mudimbe, has famously said that African knowledge, what he calls gnosis, is still hidden and waits to be discovered.[7] The claims, in the meantime, of any political party to be speaking for an authentic Africa must be taken with scepticism. In any case, all the functions Mazrui mentioned are dynamic ones. They grow and change and do so organically over time. They cannot become the conserving 'project' of one party and one generation of leadership.

With all this in mind, added to what has been happening in Zimbabwe, I asked Tsvangirai about the intellectual justifications often used by ZANU(PF).

> *Yes. The blacks have been victims. It's a victim image behind all this 'thought'. We have been victims of Arab slavery, white slavery, colonial slavery, victims of colonial subjugation. So I think, from this victim point of view, one sees an attempt to create a platform for confidence-building in Africans themselves. But I think it over-shadows the acceptance of one's own faults. Acceptance of one's own faults should overshadow this anti-white, anti-colonial, anti-slavery image that now emerges. One of the weaknesses that can be noticed in the post-independence era is that African governments, African people themselves, have taken to heaping blame on the whites, on colonialism, without accepting their own shortcomings. That is why I think pan-African solidarity has had a weakness.*

I replied that what he had said was well and good, but rather too briefly sought to summarise a complex intellectual issue. I mentioned the great amount of political and political economic work published by Zimbabwean scholars through Ibbo Mandaza's publishing house.

> *He's an apologist!*

Perhaps an apologist, I said, but nevertheless he represents part of a huge and often impressive pan-African effort to encourage research and publish it. The Mandaza effort is only part of the Dakar-based CODESRIA (Council for the Development of Social Science Research

:a) network which has brought many African scholars to the attention. There is, in crude geographical terms, a triangle lectual centres – Dakar, Dar es Salaam, and Harare – which, though the relations have become more tenuous, retains a degree of importance.

Yes, but what I mean to say is that none of this hides the fact that it's to do with the establishment of an identity. We have suffered a lot of identity problems. For a hundred years our cultures have been Westernised. The whole new society is in fact based on Western influence. At the same time, the post-independence era has given the black person in Africa some sort of identity. But the disadvantages and problems we have faced, post-independence, is that instead of focusing on our own weaknesses we have taken to passing the blame onto other people. And I think that the key question of a new renaissance, a new African identity, Africanness, should be in essence trying to say 'treat us like the rest of the world. Notwithstanding the problems we face, we will find an African solution to the African problem.' We have the capacity to do it. Yet we have not created the institutions that would be basic in taking this continent forward. We are still in the blame-game, still in a denial stage, instead of accepting that it is we who have yet to deal with even the primary issues. We are still grappling others and trying to blame other people, instead of looking at ourselves and saying 'what have we done wrong?' And the ones who have performed the greatest disservice, by not asking that, are the intellectuals.

Tsvangirai is at least consistent in his view of intellectuals. I reminded him that, eleven years ago when he was still a trade union leader, he had attacked 'progressive' intellectuals, accusing them of 'lecturing workers and peasants through journals published from their mansions in low-density suburbs', in the pages of Mandaza's own journal. Wasn't that a bit cheeky?

(Laughs) I was, yes, it may appear like a contradiction... but it was a platform with which I was associating myself. It was during the crisis of the Economic Structural Adjustment Programme. And I was actually crying out for help. The labour movement was crying out for international help. And, in dealing with this crisis we were facing, I tried to challenge our African intellectuals to offer solutions to the economic problems we were facing. That was the point I was trying to make.

I remarked that the intellectual community had been very good in criticising structural adjustment, and in pointing out its very poor cultural and social consequences, but had not come up with a viable economic solution.

No. No, they haven't. They are still tied up with the social conse-
quences. As I said, they then make excuses. Instead of offering
alternatives to the African plight they are making excuses, just like
some of us as individuals make excuses for our own failures. I just
think it's unhelpful.

I asked about the intellectual wing of the MDC itself. What did it stand
for, and was it able to be inclusive of others, or did it too take to 'lecturing workers and peasants'?

If you look at the MDC, it's more of a democratic movement. Its
character includes business elements as well as intellectual elements.
But the predominant – the predominant base – the one that defines
its values, is really the poor people. The majority of the poor people,
the ordinary poor, labour and the peasants. And of course the value
of solidarity with and among them becomes a defining value.
Solidarity, justice, liberty, freedom, equality, those are the defining
values of the MDC. I don't think that even some of the business or
capitalistic elements within the MDC would argue with these val-
ues. They wouldn't because those values define the position of the
majority.

I mentioned that the MDC intellectuals would not necessarily see
themselves outside the very same pan-African intellectual movement of which Mandaza is a part. Recent work by Ian Phimister and
Brian Raftopoulos has pointed out that South Africa's Thabo Mbeki
is also someone very conscious of, someone who buys into, that pan-
African intellectual movement. And that same movement is what the
ZANU(PF) intellectuals also buy into.

I am sure you will indeed find that the intellectual streak, the intel-
lectual vein, of Mbeki is going in almost the same way as Mandaza's
and those other intellectuals. I don't think this raises contradictions
in itself. But the sort of intellectual discourse on the continent is still
misdirecting the true focus of African renaissance. Their talk of
African renewal is still based on blame, still based on complaint, still
based on the victim image. But I think the new intellectual thrust
for a renewal of Africa should be based on offering alternatives, in
offering the African hope, in offering the basis of a new position –
one that will put Africa on a path of international credibility,
international trust and international acceptance.

I pressed Tsvangirai on this, citing Mbeki's article in which he in turn
cited the Kenyan writer, Ngugi wa Thiongo, and his book, *Decolonis-*
ing the Mind. The idea being, in Mbeki's rendition of the book anyway,
that there is a need almost to start from scratch, to reconceive Africa in
African terms, to provide in that manner the means to resist Western

pressures upon Africa that emanate from Western philosophical values alone.

This is a very narrow concept. I mean, it is once again… it is trying to say that in an age of globalisation the African alone must go back to the basic African concept. And yet the world is not going to wait for the African. It is the African who must catch up. To me, that is the challenge – the African must catch up. There are new influences of technology, information, so many other influences, and the African simply cannot exclude himself from that.

To what extent then, I asked, would Tsvangirai describe himself as a moderniser?

I think, yes, that my whole philosophy is about the future. And the future cannot continue to harp on about the past. We learn from it. I think there are lessons, there are mistakes that we have made, but I think that any leader must be able to define the future in terms of the modern challenges. So I see myself more as somebody who is trying to put the African in a more credible light, rather than an African who is always complaining about the past. I think it's time to move on. It's time to be part of the global world. Time to take on the new challenges of technology and information.

I asked whether the refusal to complain about the past was a reason why other African leaders often were unkind in their attitudes towards him.

I am sure they are. I am sure they don't find me pan-Africanist enough. I am not an apologist. I am very open in my criticism. But that criticism is not in any way meant to alienate African solidarity, African pride, not to denigrate African history. No.

I asked about Nigerian President Obasanjo's reputed critical remarks about him at the Commonwealth Heads of Government meeting in 2002.[8]

I have got a very high regard for President Obasanjo. I think we share the same mind on a number of issues. With Obasanjo we see common trends with me. We are of the same mind particularly on the crisis in Zimbabwe. He sees this as a crisis of government, a crisis of leadership – on this we certainly are of a common mind. But, if he doesn't always think I would be a good President, well (laughs)… well, I don't rely on his benevolence. There are always accusations levelled against whoever might try to sort out this mess in Zimbabwe. It's a challenge to Zimbabweans to sort out the mess and it won't be easy or perfect.

I raised the imperfections of the MDC front bench. The entire cabinet would have to 'sort out the mess', but I queried the capacities and talent of the MDC, of those who would become ministers. How modern would these modernisers actually be in terms of technocratic capacities? He was stung by this.

No. Actually this is a misrepresentation of the MDC. The depth of talent is very prevalent. Let me outline some of the capacity we have got. ZANU(PF) does not equal the capacity we have got in the MDC. In parliament we have eight lawyers. We have committees of economists – the best economic minds in the country. We have the best social practitioners in the labour movement. I certainly dispute the idea that we don't have sufficient depth to be effective modernisers.

About these 'committees of economists', I asked what their economic philosophy would be. To what extent would they seek an African version of economic social democracy?

Our economic policy is indeed based on social democratic values. We realise, of course, that redistribution alone – without production – is insufficient. Our thrust is to ensure that society creates a productive environment, but at the same time creates measures for redistribution – because we don't all have access to productive means. So I certainly believe that creating a basis for initiating, rewarding initiative, is very, very important. But also being conscious, socially conscious of the prevalence of poverty in our society is very, very important. As for 'African' social democracy, I don't believe there is a particular brand of social democracy. Everything has to be revolving around the productive forces and how you distribute their outcomes. So, for me, African, European social democracy – whatever – the fundamental issue is how do you produce and how do you distribute?

That was clear, I said, but the question couldn't be as fundamentally straightforward as that. There are international factors as well.

Yes, we're very conscious of that. The international monetary institutions, the role of the market, have become so sophisticated for a young and underdeveloped society such as we are. We have to take this into consideration. Because, I just want to explain here, in Zimbabwe today we have a government with a Reserve Bank governor who (laughs) say, 'We are on a turn-around plan'.[9] And I question myself how that turn-around plan is going to be achieved in the absence of balance-of-payments support, in the absence of a proper fiscal plan, in the absence of a proper monetary plan. I don't see anything as a planned instrument. And, yes of course, we would regard international support, international sympathy as a very

37

very critical element in turning around this economy. There's no such support right now. At the same time, with this support, you are also very susceptible to pressures.

Even with such support, I said, to help balance of payments, there would still be the problem of markets. The Zambians had taken over almost all the Zimbabwean tobacco markets internationally.

Yes, I'm conscious of all the loss of skills in our society and the loss of markets. So one must build some internal confidence. It is critical to build this. Our business people, our workers, all our entrepreneurs must realise that we have to pull up our boot straps and we have to create conditions of internal confidence so we can breathe again. We can then recapture some of the lost markets. But building internal confidence is where the question of inclusivity comes in again.

I remarked that it all sounded like an urban-based vision – business people, workers, entrepreneurs so where was the rural population and rural productivity?

That may be true of this conversation. But it's because I regard the thrust away from subsistence, to urbanisation, industrialisation, as a thrust of the MDC. In fact, I have said in another statement, 'you cannot create more peasants'. There is no society which has developed by creating more peasants than industrial workers. I certainly believe in that. It's not that I ignore the role of rural productivity. You will see that in our 'Restart' programme. If we want to tackle rural poverty there is a need to increase productivity in those areas. But that productivity is not going to come about unless you create conditions in the rural areas that will bring something much more than just a subsistence economy. And the question of support, rural sub-sectors, training of rural farmers, small-scale farmers, the question of marketing, will become part of that thrust to create the right conditions.

It is fair to comment that what Morgan Tsvangirai was saying at this point is contentious. It is broadly true that successful societies are those that have industrialised, and this would include agri-industry – not unlike what was happening on large farms in Zimbabwe before 2000. Having said that, almost all successful third world development has included a blend of peasant agriculture with agri-industry. And it is not strictly speaking true to say that industrial workers must be created in greater numbers than peasants. Firstly, it depends on the sort of industry being developed. It doesn't have to be labour-intensive, and with a relatively small population in Zimbabwe it can't be. Secondly, what is at stake is not a crude question of labour numbers but a question of sustained contribution to GNP (Gross National Product) and the possibility of sustained increased contribution to GNP. Here, rural production, involving both agri-industry and peasant agriculture, can do more than urban industry if properly planned and supported. The question is one of effectiveness, not the gross number of workers in any sector. By emphasising productivity first and foremost, Tsvangirai at least recognises this, and he recognises also the need for rural infrastructure and rural productivity. Having said that, the sheer scale of the problem of unemployment may be such that any sector, rural or urban, with absorptive capacity is going to have to be emphasised. No economy has succeeded unless it has provided livelihood. As a former trade union leader Tsvangirai has been disqualified by some people from talking in-depth about rural development, so I put it to him that one of the faults of the MDC is that it has never really had a dynamic front bench spokesman or spokeswoman on agriculture and rural productivity.

> *Yes, I think there has been some weakness. But we have a very good spokesman on general agricultural policies and land policies. I do think that the rural productivity has not come out clearly – but I do know that in the context of our 'Restart' programme it is a very substantial portion of our rural strategy.*

Very recently a labour economist, writing from a ZCTU perspective, urged a future economy with far greater outreach and support for the informal sector.[10] This was unusual in itself, especially after 40 pages of formal economic data; and is not generally a favoured strategy on the part of government planners precisely because it is not formally measurable, precisely because it cannot be precise. The informal sector has underpinned a very great deal of the Indian economy, however, and is not only highly absorptive of otherwise unabsorbable labour but is highly productive in terms both of goods and services, and of providing livelihood. It is also an alternative mode of social organisation. This sort of informal organisation is now being observed in the otherwise chaotic scenarios on some seized/resettled farms.[11] So there are new social forces being formed, and with their own modes of economic productivity. I asked Tsvangirai whether MDC thinking was catering for such forces.

> *Yes. The biggest problem is the infrastructure, which is very formal, commercial, and has been destroyed. So people have relied on more informal types of organisation. Which is wrong. This is our criticism of Mugabe's land reform programme. Because he has destroyed a very viable infrastructure that would have created a platform for rural productivity. Unfortunately what has now happened is that to formalise those informal relationships – among traditional rulers, resettled farmers – he still relies upon benevolence and patronage*

instead of market forces. He still relies on extending communal land practices into the most viable areas of our economy. And I think this is where a major problem arises.

This was Tsvangirai being very true to his sense of himself as a moderniser. I put it to him that, by contrast, perhaps Mugabe was being true to one of his original selves as a Maoist. Was this period the epoch of Mugabe's 'Cultural Revolution', the epoch of the 'New Zimbabwean' who would be the model for the 'New African'?

I think Mugabe's philosophy is more about how to retain power than about any ideological position. Because he has had variant ideological positions. You can look at the Marxist thrust, the socialist thrust, the ESAP period, the post-ESAP period, and now a period where we are back to agrarian reform. You will find that he is experimenting – experimenting – with populist positions in order to retain power. The so-called land reform – where one might have thought he was following Mao's Cultural Revolution – has been bastardised. Because who benefited from the land reform programme? It is the elite once again, as part of his system to retain power. The whole thrust has never been about empowering people. It is about empowering himself – a takeover through mass political patronage.

And I don't think Mugabe's thrust is anything to do with creating a 'New Zimbabwean' or a 'New African' along the lines of our discussions earlier. It is instead everything to do with vindictiveness, racism. In the words of Edison Zvobgo, 'we have tainted what was a glorious revolution, reducing it to some agrarian racist enterprise'. He couldn't have captured it more aptly.

It was Zvobgo (who died a few weeks after our discussions) who made great speeches against Mugabe's repressive legislation. The 'agrarian racist enterprise' speech had been as early as September 2000. At the end of January 2003 Zvobgo lambasted the public order bill as the 'most calculated and determined assault on our liberties guaranteed by the constitution'. I asked Tsvangirai why the MDC had never had someone who was such an intellectual and front bench heavyweight.

Yes. I think the reason is very simple to explain. You see, this movement comes out of the labour movement and the constitutional movement. I don't think that we have had sufficient clout within this movement, people of that intellectual depth or what you call a 'political heavyweight'. When we came upon the scene, society was ready for transition, for a change, and there was a labour movement driving that change. But there was some scepticism amongst some of the intellectuals, even some cynicism, about going forward with this new movement. Some hoped, and I think they still do, that we would fail. That there would be the emergence of another different new dynamic out of this movement. Unfortunately, we have survived, not only survived but strengthened the position of the democratic movement. Hopefully, as we move on, we will attract more of the sort that you call 'front bench heavyweights'.

We had circled back to the question of philosophy, of the battle for the mind. The battle for Zimbabwe could never have been simply a battle for hearts, but one also for minds. However seemingly far removed, the thoughts of a pan-African intellectual movement would percolate down to ordinary people, even if only by way of slogans and enemies. I related to Tsvangirai how I had found University of Zimbabwe faculty members rather neatly divided between supporters of the MDC and supporters of ZANU(PF). Some were quite desperate to retain membership in ZANU(PF). These were the cream of the nation's ability to think. I asked again why the MDC had no Zvobgos, no Simba Makonis.

It's to do with the political environment, to do with the repressive nature of the current political system. But I want to take you on to what Ibbo Mandaza's political philosophy has been. Mandaza believes there must be a 'third force' between intellectuals in the MDC and intellectuals in ZANU(PF) – led by him of course (laughs) – but what he doesn't understand is that the social activists, the women activists, all those who have been at the thrust, at the leadership of this movement, have a strong grassroots base that is actually resentful of the arrogance of the intellectuals. That's why they can't connect. You have Mandaza and others, this fringe, this fringe that feels it has been excluded from the people's democratic movement, but which is not confident of the leadership of the MDC. Yet this is the leadership with the popular support, the support of the people.

Tsvangirai had refused to blame backwards, to look at the wrongs of the past as a foundation for policies or philosophy today. He was very much for self-responsibility. He saw himself firmly as a moderniser, against any trend to reach backwards to a 'New African', and saw that the world would not wait for this new African. He also saw himself as a man of the people, and shared with them a distrust of intellectuals. And yet, looking at his bookshelves, the open books on his desk, there was clear evidence of avid reading. During a later discussion I would try again, through the medium of books he had read, to discern more deeply his own intellectual roots. At the moment he seemed to occupy a space between that of a leader of the opposition, very sure of the ground on which he stood, and a trade union leader still becoming a politician. Diplomats stationed in Harare had, over the years, com-

:d to me on Tsvangirai's constantly rising capacity to see and do s in a thoughtful political way. No one had ever doubted his foun- n idealism, his moral sense and outrage, and his sheer courage. This had always conveyed itself to his supporters by a charisma which very few in Zimbabwe could match. He had held together a broad-based coalition of largely urban elements and his party, despite assertions to the contrary, has its own very strong intellectual wing – itself still learning its way forward in terms of applying thought to policy. With all of this, however, could he ever be more than a leader of the opposition? Did he have the capacity to be President? And what sort of President? The Latin American populists, from Argentina's Peron to Hugo Chavez in Venezuela today, were hugely problematic leaders for both their nations and the international community. In neighbouring Zambia, the example of the trade union leader turned President on an initial wave of popular acclaim, Frederick Chiluba, was both depressing and squalid. At the height of Chiluba's very poor Presidency, Zambians would joke with Zimbabweans, offering to trade Chiluba for Tsvangirai – one trade union leader for another – on the grounds that Tsvangirai would be better. Would he be better? Treason charges and the conditions of his bail have meant that Tsvangirai has not been able to visit the outside world to influence and impress international political and diplomatic opinion. It means that the outside world has no real sense of him and has to rely on embassy reports. What, however, is Tsvangirai's sense of that outside world? What sort of President would he be for the world? After all, he would walk the halls of the African Union, the Commonwealth and the United Nations. He would negotiate with the IMF in Washington and meet the exceedingly judgmental leaders of Europe. He would have to learn how to deal with the concealing leaders of China and Japan. I wanted to explore these things in my next conversation with him.

Notes

1. Ali A. Mazrui, *Cultural Forces in World Politics*, London: James Currey, 1990, pp. 7–8.
2. Ibid., pp. 132–7.
3. For example, Molefi Kete Asante, *The Afrocentric Idea*, Philadelphia: Temple University Press, 1987. Marimba Ba, *Yurugu: An African-Centred Critique of European Cultural Thought and Behavior*, Trenton: Africa World Press, 1994.
4. Barry Hallen, *A Short History of African Philosophy*, Bloomington: Indiana University Press, 2002.
5. Achille Mbembe, 'Power and Obscenity in the Post-Colonial Period: the Case of Cameroon', in James Manor (ed.), *Rethinking Third World Politics*, London: Longman, 1991, p. 166.
6. Ibid., p. 170.
7. V.Y. Mudimbe, *The Invention of Africa: Gnosis, Philosophy, and the Order of*

Knowledge, Bloomington: Indiana University Press, 1988, p. 186.

8. Obasanjo is said to have confided to the Commonwealth Secretary-General that he did not think Tsvangirai had enough capability and skill to be even a junior member of the Nigerian cabinet.

9. This was a reference to the headline in *The Herald* (Harare), 28 July 2004, in which the Governor of the Reserve Bank of Zimbabwe, Gideon Gono, had indeed proclaimed an economic turn-around. To be fair to Gono, he had in his tenure as Governor worked to stabilise the economy – although at a very low level and a very precarious one, and one in which hyper-inflation was still a significant factor. Nevertheless, the economy was no longer in dramatic freefall – although it was still falling. It was certainly not rising at the end of July 2004. Nor would it rise on the basis of past productivity. Across the border in Zambia, tobacco farmers had captured the bulk of Zimbabwe's former markets and had already been receiving investment and technical inputs to raise Zambian productivity from the cheap end of the tobacco market to the high-quality end. In 2003, Zimbabwe became the world's fastest-shrinking economy. For an overview of that year, see Brian MacGarry, 'The Zimbabwe Economy in 2003', *Zimbabwe Review (Britain Zimbabwe Society)*, 04/2, May 2004.

10. Godfrey Kanyenze, 'The Zimbabwean Economy 1980–2003: a ZCTU perspective', in David Harold-Barry (ed.), *Zimbabwe: The Past is the Future*, Harare: Weaver Press, 2004, p. 147.

11. Joseph Chaumba, Ian Scoones and William Wolmer, 'New Politics, New Livelihoods: Agrarian Change in Zimbabwe', *Review of African Political Economy*, No. 98, 2003.

Internationalism & Reconciliation

The world of international diplomacy, although committed to gentlemanly manners, is a viper's nest of ungentlemanly conduct. There are exceptions. I think the former French Foreign Minister Dominique de Villepin's UN speech against war with Iraq will stand as a masterpiece of political judgement and rare morality.[1] To an alarming extent, however, political judgement triumphs over morality. In the case of Zimbabwe, it must be said that a lot of Western support for Morgan Tsvangirai is simply the 'anyone but Mugabe' syndrome. And, when it comes down to it, this is not simply because Mugabe is perceived as a tyrant – he is – but because he has destabilised a region in which the West had great hopes as an integrated economic unit. Again, the view of the West is more nuanced than that bald statement. The West would like southern Africa to develop as an example to the rest of the continent, and southern Africa has the capacity to do this. There is a genuine normative, or moral, hope that Africa will turn a corner from the south up. Simultaneously, if the West seeks an expanded international economic community in which the global flow of capital can be enriched then southern Africa is a good addition to the fully-fledged community; or was, until Zimbabwe began its precipitate slide downwards. Frankly, when it comes to an alternative to Mugabe, the West would be as happy, if not happier, if ZANU(PF)'s Simba Makoni became President. An economic technocrat, a reforming moderate, someone who offers continuity with the ZANU(PF) past but also offers an accommodation with the MDC in the future, with Makoni the strategists in the West can tick off all their boxes.

Moreover, Tsvangirai's internal exile, his inability since the treason charges to travel outside Zimbabwe, has not helped his international cause. In addition, as noted above, my first conversations with him in October 2000 recorded exceedingly abrupt and, in my opinion, ill-considered views of international institutions and personalities such as the Commonwealth's Don McKinnon and the UN's Kofi Annan. It is not that these people are 'good' or even effective. It is a question of how to deal with such people, how to garner support with and through them.

To many outside Zimbabwe, Tsvangirai's mission and his policies seem very Zimbabwe-bound. No one knows what an MDC foreign policy would actually look like. It is not just for 'good' or Machiavellian reasons that the West has an interest in leadership in Zimbabwe, the West also has an interest in what sort of participant Zimbabwe would be in the world community. Here, the MDC's projection of itself has been completely invisible. This might now be changing. Recently, Kofi Annan has delivered himself of quite stinging rebukes to African Union leaders, stressing the need for democracy, democratic change, transparency and constitutional governance – and pointing out that no one has the right to cling to power permanently. This has not been lost on Morgan Tsvangirai. The Annan remarks had encouraged and delighted him.

Annan was contemptuous. In fact he was almost like some headmaster dealing with delinquent children (laughs), very critical of some of the leaders who don't want to give up power. It was a very significant moment.[2] There is now a significant observation that the conflicts, the degradation in Africa, are because of an absence of democratic leadership. And in this region, I have seen a movement in which standards for elections are a significant agenda for the next SADC Heads of State meeting.[3] So my earlier cynicism around the international approach to the Zimbabwe crisis has, I think, moved on. There have been positive changes in bringing the Zimbabwe issue forwards. Recent comments by the Americans, by the European Union, on the Zimbabwean by-elections and on the food situation mean that there is now a much more co-ordinated international approach. There are differences here and there, but I think there is a common theme.

I asked whether it was truly so co-ordinated. I noted that at the recent Commonwealth summit in Abuja, December 2003, although it was finally agreed to extend the suspension of Zimbabwe – with Zimbabwe on the same day unilaterally withdrawing – the Commonwealth leaders really had to labour to arrive at this decision.

But eventually they did. And I think it was the leadership of Nigeria that eventually reconciled the two opposing sides.

Nigeria's having to push, Annan's having to rebuke African leaders, I asked whether all this meant that movement towards honest democracy is not yet voluntary.

We haven't reached that stage. There has only been one sustained direct criticism of Mugabe on the part of the African Union. As for the Commonwealth, Mugabe sought to evade the criticism of the Commonwealth by blaming it on the white Commonwealth – rather than admit that it was a principled stand by the whole body.

And, as for the MDC approach, there has been criticism that we were ready to run to the EU, run to the Americans, to take action on Zimbabwe, run to them and say they were ignoring the Africans. I think it's a criticism well taken. We have been working and trying to make sure that the African agenda becomes the defining thrust in confronting Mugabe – not an EU or American agenda – and we have been starting with our diplomatic initiative with Mbeki, with the leaders of the region, and with the African Union. We are sending delegations to West Africa. So we have been concentrating more on trying to gain political voices in Africa.

At this stage I said that he, Tsvangirai, could not personally lead any of those delegations, and it was important for the MDC to have someone who could. I said, pointedly, that Sekai Holland had been a consistent disaster internationally.

No, but we have since dropped her…

Only after a long time, I interjected.

After a long time. I had not put myself in a strategic position of defining the diplomatic agenda. Now that I have done that, we have seen more briefings with the diplomatic community in Zimbabwe. We have been more focused and strategically chosen representatives of our missions outside the country. We know who has got what skills and we have had a more focused message internationally. For instance, we realise that the crisis of legitimacy is at the centre of the crisis of government in Zimbabwe. We are saying that the resolution of the crisis can only be undertaken by the next elections that are coming. So we are mobilising national and international opinion around creating conditions for a free and fair election. These are the March parliamentary elections – because we realise that any legitimate outcome may actually resolve the political crisis of legitimacy. And so our thrust diplomatically has to be to persuade people to focus on that. And I think opinion is indeed beginning to coalesce around that.

The shift in focus is indeed a maturing for the MDC. Previously its diplomacy had been almost plaintive, pleading for external action on Zimbabwe; or hectoring, demanding external action. Sekai Holland, as foreign spokesperson, had never developed the sort of diplomatic skills required for the international circuit. To be fair to her, since 2000, almost all the Zimbabwean ambassadors had adopted a fortress-like defence from behind the walls of their embassies, emerging only to engage in a ZANU(PF) style of haranguing their international audiences, lecturing them as if they were addressing political rallies. That being the case, however, the international community could see no difference between the representatives of the government and the opposition. Sekai Holland had been a personal friend of Tsvangirai and he had been reluctant to dismiss her. But if there was now a new focus, what was it? Was it simply a more nuanced diplomacy about Zimbabwe? Did Morgan Tsvangirai, if not the MDC as yet, have a broader foreign policy?

First of all I think there are things the MDC should be able to say: that Zimbabwe must be part of the international community, adhering to international standards of confidence, of democracy, human rights, and of course free elections. The world has now become globalised. That we should find a niche market in that global environment. This, rather than the international community defining what Zimbabwe should be. We find our niche rather than anyone else finding it for us. But I think we are more influenced by the plight of the third world, the plight of Africa. We are more influenced by our position amongst the disadvantaged communities of the world.

I asked about other areas of the third world, outside Africa, where there are problems not only of poverty but of internationalised violence – as in the Middle East.

What will be required – first and foremost – in the Middle East is to take a stand. To say that the right of the Palestinians to self-rule is not negotiable. But at the same time we will be able to say that the existence of Israel also has to be guarded. But it cannot be guaranteed by the exclusion of the Palestinians. This has really been at the basis of conflict in the Middle East, right? In Africa we also have conflicts, ethnic conflicts, and these really should end.

Would, then, an MDC-led Zimbabwe be active in peacekeeping? I pointed out the extreme logistical difficulties troops from neighbouring Zambia had experienced in a long, proud, but problem-strewn history of peacekeeping.

Oh yes, I think peacekeeping will be one of our major thrusts. We will certainly be – in Africa we will be at the forefront in promoting peacekeeping ventures. Because we don't believe Africa can develop with all these conflicts rampant all over the continent. These conflicts are unnecessary. I think we should demonstrate that we have come out of conflict, out of the legacy of ethnic conflict, and then we should actually strengthen rather than weaken our nation-states. And, yes, there are challenges about how to do it. But the challenge of a peacekeeping effort is a combination of peacebuilding as well as peacekeeping. I think the thrust in African conflict should be peacebuilding. The political and diplomatic effort is complemen-

tary to any military peacekeeping. The political effort must precede the military effort. But I think that sending out your people for peacekeeping efforts under-equipped or ill-equipped, I think it's irresponsible.

I wanted to get onto more topical ground. Tsvangirai was saying all the right things, but they were very generalised things. If there was a preparedness for well-equipped military peacekeeping, then it had to be part of a doctrine of military preparedness in general. So I asked him about military preparedness, military philosophy, military commitment. Would Zimbabwe have a purely defensive military? Would it have a military capable of peacekeeping and, if so, could it be upgraded to be capable also of more aggressive external intervention?

Our philosophy will guide the defence forces. For instance, peace, law and order must be the purview of the police force. I think that the defence forces must be more for defence than offence. And when it comes to peacekeeping, one of our philosophies is of course to reduce our defence expenditure but keep a versatile, well-equipped, well-trained, well-supported but smaller defence force. And to use it to take up any peacekeeping efforts as defined by the United Nations. We are not going to undertake adventurist peacekeeping efforts, or so-called conflict-prevention efforts like we did in the Congo. It's not part of our philosophy. I think it's not in our national interest. Of course, our defence policy will actually be defined by our national interest.

I asked about military and senior political plunder in the Congo. Many young soldiers died so that more senior people could become rich. This has been internationally recognised and rather carefully monitored. There are lists of names, the companies used by these names, how much has been plundered. In the new Zimbabwe, led by the MDC, would there be inclusiveness for the senior military plunderers?

First and foremost, the culture of plunder in the military is going to require a long-term, not a short-term, solution. But I think that, even in the medium-term, you will be able to weed out some of the culprits in the defence forces in order to create a new philosophy in the army that the culture of service is not synonymous with the culture of plunder. The temptation is that when you plunder outside resources you enrich yourselves, but you also become a source of internal destabilisation. You think you are above the law. There are some in the military high command who have had access to unearned wealth, ill-begotten wealth, and you wonder whether they are actually professional military people or just asset-strippers. So I think that is going to take a long time. Our philosophy is not to destabilise, because if it is done in a rushed way – if you have a Truth and

*Justice Commission for instance – a lot of people will not escape it.
It was not only plunder but also murder, including murder inter-
nally. So I think that part of our rationale really has to include
phasing out this crop of military leadership, but without making it
a sudden and abrupt thing.*

I noted that Tsvangirai had used the term, Truth and Justice Commission, rather than Truth and Reconciliation Commission as was the
case in South Africa. I asked whether a Truth and Justice Commission
would go beyond what occurred in South Africa.

*We have said that we need not only truth to be told, but at some
stage you need justice. It goes beyond South Africa. Because I think
our philosophy is that you cannot hide the truth. At the same time,
you cannot ignore the plight of the victims, the cries of the victims,
neither should the perpetrators be allowed to get away with it.
Because if you allow it now, what will stop future generations pursuing the same philosophy? I think we must draw a line, that perpetrators of human rights abuses cannot be allowed to get away with
it. I know it's difficult to establish who are the culprits because of the
command structure and command system in the military. But I do
think there are culprits roaming the country with impunity. As for
the non-military, political plunderers, I am sure that you can't have
a national healing process unless you resolve what has happened.
Look at the ruling elite. The crimes they have committed in acquir-
ing their assets. It's beyond... You cannot heal the nation until that
is resolved.*

No inclusiveness without justice then. I asked whether that was an
apt summary. But I added that Tsvangirai was establishing quite an
agenda: economic recovery, political development, military reform,
and what would be a very emotional and fraught process of healing
with justice.

*It is difficult. But let me say that we are setting ourselves goals. We
know we are inheriting a fractured society. We are going to inherit
a traumatised society. We are going to inherit a society that has been
denied equal opportunity to develop, one in which there was heavy
patronage for political purposes.*

I remarked that, in South Africa, even with a Truth and Reconciliation Commission, and not a Truth and Justice Commission, the process required all the moral charisma of giant figures such as Mandela
and Archbishop Tutu. I asked if Zimbabwe had people of such moral
stature.

*I am sure there are. There are very credible people in this country.
You have people who have excelled themselves and tried to fight*

injustice. There are some clerics who have excelled themselves and a couple of notable academics. I think this process would indeed need somebody whom people have confidence in. It is very important to establish, to identify, such a person. You don't want him to be too legalistic. You want it to be a real healing process.

I immediately objected that if it was not 'too legalistic', then there was a danger of imperfect and unfair legal process.

Yes, I recognise that. I take note of that. I think there should be some balance, but you do need to do this with balance.

I thought it best to end the conversation at this stage. Tsvangirai was getting tired. The pollen-laden tree was having an effect on him. It was clear that he had matured a great deal in matters of foreign policy and his thinking on international matters. But it was also clear that this was not a Tsvangirai speciality. He needed foreign policy specialists around him, and the fact that he had taken it upon himself to help formulate the MDC foreign policy I took to be indicative, no matter what his protests on the matter, of a lack of talent in that direction at least within the top ranks of the MDC. African countries seem quite notoriously determined to insert mediocre people into the position of foreign minister. By comparison, at time of writing, the immediate past French foreign minister, Dominique de Villepin, is an educated technocrat whose 'hobby' is writing voluminous tomes on French symbolist poetry; the US Secretary of State, Colin Powell, is a former General of some distinction – not in enriching himself or supervising a botched peacekeeping operation, but in running a hugely complex military machine in war as well as peace; the US National Security Advisor, Condoleezza Rice, was a professor in international politics at Stanford. They inhabit a world which is wicked and, no doubt, add to its wicked procedures and sometimes its outcomes. But they also inhabit a world that is not for amateurs. In any case, Tsvangirai really can't be both President and foreign minister. There are enough specialist difficulties in either one of those positions to be getting on with. Tsvangirai and I were going to start on another round of discussions the next day. I was determined to uncover more of him – his personality, his political philosophy, his sense of truth and justice, his sense of democracy, and even some more insights on foreign policy. And we had not even skirted around truly sensitive issues such as the question of treason. And tomorrow I was going to arrange my own driver and car. I did not want to ride around anymore in improvised armour. It is a fierce view, but I do not think that even in the third world you have to improvise all the time. So, on the morrow, I was going to be fiercer with Tsvangirai.

Notes

1. I have celebrated this in my new work: Stephen Chan, *Out of Evil: New International Politics and Old Doctrines of Wa*r, London: I.B. Tauris and Ann Arbor: University of Michigan Press, 2005.
2. This was Kofi Annan's Address to the African Union Summit, Addis Ababa, 6 July 2004. The speech in fact attracted most international headlines for its concern over slaughter and dispossession in Darfur, Sudan. However, Annan did indeed go on to speak about democracy in Africa. It is probably an exaggeration to call the speech headmasterly. However, Annan was quite emphatic in delivering himself of lines such as: 'Let us remember that constitutions are for the long term benefit of society, not the short term goals of the ruler'. The speech is available on the African Union website.
3. This was well forecast at the end of July by Tsvangirai because, indeed, at the SADC summit in Mauritius on 17 August 2004 the Heads of State were intent on delivering a stinging rebuke of Mr Mugabe. The Mauritian Prime Minister said: 'Really free and fair elections mean not only an independent electoral commission, but also include freedom of assembly and absence of physical harassment by the police or any other entity, freedom of the press and access to national radio and television, and external and credible observation of the whole electoral process.' *The Guardian* (London), 18 August 2004, p. 14. With Namibia's Sam Nujoma shortly stepping down, Zimbabwe will be the region's only state without a change in leadership since independence.

Perseverance

I need not have bothered. Overnight it seemed as if Morgan Tsvangirai had also decided to engage with the project of expressing himself more fully. The offending tree was still shedding its pollen; Tsvangirai was wearing a striped business shirt, just back from MDC Headquarters in Harvest House, and he began by talking about his latest MDC newsletter in which he had expressed the frustration of campaigning. Everywhere he had recently gone he had been met by harassment or obstruction. Either a gang of ZANU(PF) militants would be waiting, or a hall booking had been mysteriously cancelled. There had also been the axe attack at the beginning of July.[1] I asked him about how he coped with the sheer, grinding attrition of it all.

Well, I think I have been naturally an optimist. But there are times, I must say, when you feel that in spite of your efforts the obstacles become too daunting. As the leader of a party confronted by these frustrations I operate on the basis of the suppression of my own individual frustrations. Whether I deserve it or not, I try to portray a positive image in spite of the frustration.

I suggested that, even so, he must have his private moments when he comes home and just feels that life outside is overwhelming. I imagined him shutting himself away in his study, sitting in the same armchair, back hunched, chin in his hands. How do you address these things, I asked, within yourself in your private moments?

In most cases I have found that having a loving family, a loving wife, a supportive wife, a supportive family background – not just your wife and your kids, but the whole family – well, you need that support. It's an anchor which you have in order to continue during these frustrations. It's not just a question of putting on a brave face. I am actually a calm person, very calm. I don't get easily excited about matters. Maybe because I have been beaten down and I have had to work hard, and I think over the years it has been an enforcing of that character.

I smiled: 'So you've been toughened up?'

Toughened up. You can say that. I don't get easily excited. In fact I find myself in most cases the calming factor in a situation in which you have to deal with an excited youth – being the nature of our party – frustrated youth and I think their agitation for more radical action.

I said that the consensus among external observers was that the MDC youth wing was much calmer than the ZANU(PF) youth wing.

Yes it is. It is because we have constantly addressed the issue of youth excitement and agitation. If we had not done that things would really have gone out of control. So I think that I do relate to this calming effect as part of dealing with the crisis.

I mentioned that former President Kaunda of Zambia used to refer constantly to his Christian faith. So I asked if he also had some kind of philosophy or faith.

No, I don't think that I am a religious person, although of course I am not an atheist. (Laughs.) But I believe in the spiritual, in the inner spiritual calmness, so I think that is a spiritual influence. I am not religious. But at the same time you find that I am not an atheist.

I laughed in turn and said he sounded like an oriental person. He laughed back and said he didn't know about that. Somehow, however, he was dealing with terrible frustrations, and not just frustrations in the normal sense. He was dealing with moments of great danger. I asked about the axe attack at the beginning of July.

Yes, I have had to confront... in fact, I have had to miss death by a whisker a couple of times in my political career over the last five or six years. There was a time when I was in the ZCTU which was very, almost close – when I was overthrown on the tenth floor of a building [here Tsvangirai is referring to the 1998 incident, recalled in endnote 1]. *They expected to intimidate me. Obviously it was intended to intimidate [or actually to kill; perhaps Tsvangirai preferred to interpret it as intimidation to keep his calm perspective], but we came out very strong from it. There was a time during my presidential campaign when I was attacked in Bindura, I was attacked in Pechwe. This latest one in Mvurwi. In these moments you realise that the party is under siege. The democratic movement is under siege. What inspires me to continue is actually the support of the people. When I go out there and talk to the people and I see they have invested their hope in me as an individual and the movement as an organisation, it keeps me motivated to do even more to achieve the goal, and that's what drives me more, so that I get inner inspiration to continue with the struggle. Because there are so many people who are dependent – it's almost like a life or death choice. If we don't succeed it's almost like the country can never be safe.*

I asked whether we could concentrate for a moment on those people immediately around him, especially at moments such as the axe attack – the bodyguards who put themselves into the line of fire; those same well-dressed and polite young men who open and close the gates for me. I asked Tsvangirai what he says to them. Surely, I said, they above all must have moments of immense frustration and want to counter violence with violence.

Yes. They know the risks. I think collectively they get inspiration from my continued calmness and continued leadership. They know they are not getting anything out of it, except to continue committed to the ultimate goal. They know what sacrifices I make. But they put up with it in a very heartening manner. And maybe it's out of their training, but it's also out of their experience. They are the frontline image of me. Sometimes when I go out I actually have to deal with their anxieties, because they also get frustrated and sometimes they rough people up and I have to say, 'look, you don't have to do that'. So I don't believe that in situations like this you need to show your frustrations to everyone, you have to control yourself. And sometimes they get so agitated that the impression they give, by roughing up an individual, it's actually a reflection on me. So, as far as I am concerned, they have to deal with the people in the same way as I deal with the people.

I asked what they would have done if they had caught one of those trying to take an axe in the direction of Tsvangirai.

Obviously they will rough him up. But under those circumstances it's not a choice. It's just not a choice. You are confronting a real threat, and they have to deal with it in a manner which they feel is effective.

I asked if we could talk about other people around him, and about Tsvangirai's efforts to calm them. There is a group of very senior MDC leaders, and there have been many reports of splits among them. This, I said, is not just *Herald* propaganda, but political reportage from embassies to their governments; reportage in many of the most respected newspapers in the world. Even the BBC on 16 July 2004 reported discord within the MDC. It identified two key factions, one led by MDC National Chairman, Isaac Matongo, who has a trade union background; and one led by Welshman Ncube, supposedly representing an intellectual faction. Others have described the factions in ethnic terms, with Karangas led by Matongo, and many Ndebele opposed to them. In any case, Tsvangirai was reported to have been involved in a 'verbal punch-up' at Harvest House with Matongo on 13 July 2004.[2] Tsvangirai agreed with me that the reports were not propaganda, and I added that British ministers had been closely briefed on these divisions. I had lunched with the Foreign Office minister responsible for Africa, and his chief adviser, shortly before visiting Zimbabwe, and had been amazed how closely informed they were.

> *But let me say, yes, I admit... I have to admit that we are a young party with a number of old lives... but we have a clear focus and a clear objective. There is sometimes an attempt to turf-fight because those – the party emerged from the grassroots, trade unions – and they feel they own it. It's a base. But they see sometimes an intellectual arrogance, which really gets frustrating because it's more to do with over-control, over-bureaucratisation, and you know trade unions are outgoing, they are more mass-based, they are more agitational and all that. And yet you see the character of some of our intellectuals, and they need things to be in the boardroom, in discussing rules and procedures and all that. But it's a tension that we manage well.*

I remarked that his comment about being 'more agitational' almost perfectly described Isaac Matongo.

> *(Laughs.) Yes, yes, I mean I know those traits. But the fact that the party has not only survived, but has succeeded beyond any ordinary expectation, is because we have managed those tensions.*

This reply by Tsvangirai was fair enough; there are tensions within ZANU(PF) as well: and within the British Labour Party, with Tony Blair and Gordon Brown seemingly always being rumoured at loggerheads and Brown intent on seizing the succession for himself. In the case of the MDC however there was a critical difference. The very day that Tsvangirai and I were having this conversation was 29 July 2004. Until a postponement at the last minute, it was the very day on which the verdict in his treason trial was to have been announced. A lot of the faction-fighting and jockeying for position within the MDC was precisely because many thought Tsvangirai would, on this very day, have been sent to prison. There had been serious issues involved in the turf-fight. The key issue would have been over who would lead the party.

> *Yes, I don't deny the fact that there may be stakes, positions at stake, stakes involved in positioning as to who controls the party beyond a certain stage. But I think there is, beyond that, a real conflict around the condescending – and yet it is just a matter of defining skill and depth of skill – and this is interpreted sometimes*

as a condescending attitude of 'we know better' – you know, that kind of attitude. And you must understand that some intellectuals are only so-called. We have people with university training but that does not mean necessarily that they are intellectuals when they assert themselves as such.

I didn't want the reportage, with its cleavage between intellectuals and unionists, to dominate the discussion about party problems; so I asked Tsvangirai about when he went to Harvest House – as he had been that very morning – and he presided over meetings with the very people at the centre of rumours around the table. Did he ever have misgivings about having to unify them?

I have to discipline certain extreme emotions, frustrations. I have to keep on the focus. I have to maintain the leadership focused on the agenda of the party. Remember that this party is so huge, it grew so big so quickly that literally the fault-lines are unavoidable for a party of our size. It's unavoidable, and I accept it. It's natural that those should be there and people should express their frustrations – and then we deal with them.

I smiled and said that this was the art of Morgan Tsvangirai, the calm centre of the storm once again.

Yes, you can say that. Without this, you see… we are coming from a society which has dictatorial tendencies. (Laughs.) And we are trying to portray ourselves as developing a democratic ethos, a democratic culture, to confront this dictatorship with a democratic alternative. It is very difficult, because internal democracy in a young, fragile organisation can also be a source of weakness. At the same time, being too dictatorial may actually put us back again within the same tendencies we are fighting against.

But let me go back to your theme about divisions. Those have not affected the organisation, have not stopped the party from going forward. They have not affected the party from portraying cohesion within the leadership – right? And we have instituted over the past five years methods of dealing with our own internal contradictions that may arise from time to time.

By talking about party divisions we had entered the realm of the treason trial. This was the day on which the verdict was to have been announced – until its postponement only days before.[3] The verdict was, at that time, impossible to predict. I asked Tsvangirai how he had prepared himself for what could have been the worst.

Well, first and foremost, I have already concluded that either an acquittal or a conviction provides the MDC and the democratic movement with a very great opportunity to mobilise people against this dictatorship. The MDC leadership has already decided that, if the president should be arrested, then it's not a question about the president being arrested. Instead I become a symbol of political mobilisation. I think it's a good rallying point. So for me, personally, whether an acquittal or a conviction, it still provides momentum to the democratic struggle.

I replied that he had carefully not said anything about his personal feelings, his personal imagination about the consequences.

I am anxious as a person. Should a conviction happen, with all its consequences, it will have a direct impact on me personally, a direct impact on my family, and it will have a very serious impact on the unity of the party. But I'm not trying to put the party before my own personal interest. I am sure my family will be devastated by such an outcome. Of course, the political consequences of my own personal misfortune will create even more fissures in the party...

I added that, from a prison cell, he would not be able to control those fissures as he had in the past.

I can't control them, what happens outside. I may have a moral impact, but certainly I can't control what happens outside.

Tsvangirai was being very blunt and forthright. I decided to push a little further. I said that he might have been facing capital punishment. What feelings of trepidation might have run through his head?

Well, it's... they bring emotions about a tragic end. I will not be scared as such, because I feel it's not because I am guilty, but because – I don't go around with a guilty conscience – because I believe I have been persecuted. I have been prosecuted and persecuted for taking a stand against dictatorship. I just happen to be one of the victims. I also knew the risks involved. When I joined politics against Robert Mugabe I knew exactly the risks and pitfalls, and I prepared myself for any consequences of this political struggle. So, should capital punishment be the ultimate, the ultimate decision, then so be it.

I remarked that these were very impressive and incredibly brave words. But, since he was not religious, what does he read that inspires him towards such a moral stand? What are Tsvangirai's influences?

Well, you know, every person has got mentors in life. You know... you know, I have been in prison, I have been in and out of prison a couple of times for my political beliefs. I know I am being persecuted. But there have been so many who have been persecuted on behalf of the people. For Zimbabwe to be independent, people had to make personal sacrifice. So, right, for us to get freedom and our democracy in this country we have to go through another phase again to confront a very vicious and brutal tyranny. Apparently I am at the forefront, I am at the head of this reality. I have to keep on confronting. Otherwise, if I don't keep pushing in spite of all these problems that we face then we will betray the whole struggle. And there are people like Mandela. I mean... look... Mandela was in prison for 27 years! I can't imagine that one would go behind bars for 27 years! And he came out with a very strong, unwavering, high moral standing, to the extent that the perpetrators of his arrest became actually just midgets. You know? And he became the moral... well, you just cannot confront that.

As for other mentors, well, beyond the political – because at the political level I don't look beyond Mandela – you know, at the family level I always regarded my grandmother as somebody who represented life, and it was a difficult life. She was widowed with two young daughters, my mother and my aunt. She remarried, but the amount of personal fortitude she displayed had a great impact on me. I was not living with her, so I was not brought up by her, but I always looked up to her as someone who had a very high moral fortitude.

There have been other influences but, in terms of non-family mentoring, it has to be Mandela who rises above everybody else. Those 27 years...

And my father is, I would say in terms of character and determination, somebody I believe has had an influence on my own character – but also in an extreme sense, because he was somebody who was inflexible. And I always said, no, this man, if he is determined to do something like that, then he doesn't waver, he just goes at it, right or wrong he just goes at it.

I asked how Morgan Tsvangirai could be determined and flexible at the same time.

I don't know.

Because, I said, his father was characteristic of most people.

Yes, but you need some degree of flexibility. You know, in a leadership position you need it. If you are inflexible, then you are not open to other ideas. You just go on your own. That's a source of real hard-nosed dictatorship, I think.

I mentioned that every time I came to see him he had his nose in a book. Had any authors inspired him?

Yes, yes. As you can see (laughs), most of my books are to do with leadership biographies. I enjoy leadership books, historical books, those sorts of things. I believe some people's life experiences can have a direct or at least indirect impact on you. I was reading Giuliani's book, the mayor at the time of 9/11, this New York mayor, and it was very impressive. One on Mandela, one on Walter Sisulu. This one's by Madeleine Albright. All sorts, some collected, some are borrowed, but those are the kinds of books. I read a lot. I am an avid reader. Read widely. And I think that has helped me because, as you can imagine, I am not an academic – but I have read so widely that I can articulate myself on the contemporary subjects, about contemporary issues. You can tell me about issues in whatever part of the world and I am quite familiar with them.

I said that the Zimbabwe Book Fair was beginning very shortly. The preceding conference was beginning the next day (in fact it was about pan-Africanism), and then there would be all the stalls in the park with people selling books from all over Africa. I asked if there were any Zimbabwean authors he had read and admired.

Oh yes. There's Tsitsi Dangarembga. She wrote this book about the role of women.[4] A very good author. A very good writer.

Dambudzo Marechera is very good. I read The House of Hunger, *and it was very, very good.[5]*

I mentioned that he had very controversial taste in liking Marechera so much.

Well, I've also heard Dambudzo Marechera speak. That man was so gifted. Emotionally gifted and it was wasted, you know. He could have gone so many places if he could have pursued his literary career. I think he was exceptional.

I was much taken by Tsvangirai's remark. Marechera's work has been so evocative that other Zimbabwean writers, especially academic ones, have used quotations from his work as epigrams to introduce their own books.[6] And it is evocative for very good reasons. *The House of Hunger* is very deliberately disillusioned with the 'black heroes of our time' (p. 12). It is neither nationalist nor pan-Africanist, but is instead a recitation of individual mental anguish. And it is an anguish that may have been caused by the possession of Marechera by a hostile ngozi or spirit.[7] Rather than the spirit world endorsing him, as ZANU(PF) was able to claim of its guerrilla forces,[8] the spirit world tormented him. He developed a terrible stutter, was unable to concentrate on his studies at Oxford and, finally, almost as emblematic of a new tragedy about to strike post-independence Zimbabwe, he died of AIDS.

Beyond that, Tsvangirai was not prepared to pretend to be familiar with what he had not read. The novels were clearly among the books that he said he borrowed, for the shelves were very much full of historical works and what he called 'leadership' works. The Mandela autobiography was obviously there because of Tsvangirai's huge admiration for a man who had suffered so many years but had not cheapened his soul with bitterness. The autobiographies of Giuliani and Albright were a surprise. Guiliani's account of pulling a traumatised city around after the attack of 9/11 might perhaps provide a metaphor for what Tsvangirai wanted to do for Zimbabwe; but the Albright book – a surprisingly literate book by the former US National Security Adviser – might have played some role in deepening Tsvangirai's previously sketchy approach to foreign affairs. And there were all the works on Zimbabwean history adorning the shelves.

Tsvangirai is not an academic, and he admitted as much; nor does he see himself as an intellectual. He reads widely but not systematically in the way one would in developing a theory, a philosophy, or even an ideology such as what pan-Africanism has now become. But it was clear he did not read indiscriminately either, but as one consumed by Zimbabwe and the question of what qualities were required to lead a battered country. I was getting an idea about Tsvangirai's familial and his intellectual roots. One doesn't have to be a pan-Africanist, be engaged in a debate on pan-Africanism, or be on the 'intellectual' wing of a party to be well-read and thoughtful. There are clear difficulties with pan-Africanism slipping into an Africa–essentialism, but this is not what Tsvangirai is concerned about. He is concerned with his familial values and those of Mandela. He is concerned about inflexibility and suffering. Apart from the leadership books it was very revealing that the two novels he enthused over, *Nervous Conditions* and *The House of Hunger*, were both about psychologically fractured people. These are, as it were, books for a doctor about to treat a patient. And, since Marechera had died of AIDS, it seemed a good moment to turn the conversation to the HIV/AIDS pandemic that will kill many more people than any dictator.

Notes

1. This attack was variously reported. Both Reuters and Agence France Presse, 2 July 2004, reported the incident differently. Reuters quoted an MDC spokesman, William Bango, as saying 'this was a clear assassination attempt on our president', whereas Agence France Presse reported the matter as a serious attack on MDC supporters generally, but which Tsvangirai was able to escape uninjured. The French agency did recall that, in February 2004, both Tsvangirai and his wife had been attacked while campaigning together. According to Dow Jones International News, 2 July 2004, David Coltart said: 'It is an exaggeration to say it was an assassination attempt against him, but he could certainly have been killed.' Many MDC supporters were injured and the implication was that the violence was indiscriminate and only good luck, or good protection, secured Tsvangirai's

escape. The same report recalled that, in 1998, ZANU(PF) militants had beaten Tsvangirai over the head with a piece of furniture and tried to throw him out of a tenth-floor window. Angus Shaw, writing for Associated Press, 2 July 2004, said that Tsvangirai 'ran from a hail of stones, taking shelter in his armour-protected car'. This was probably a calculated and vicious effort at intimidation, rather than assassination – but, reflecting back on the news reports, I guess I was reassured that the armour did work.

2. The most pertinent Zimbabwean source is the *Financial Gazette* (Harare), 15 July 2004.

3. The postponement was reported as being due to various causes. One was the success of Tsvangirai's lawyers in demanding to be able to review the transcripts of all evidence presented in court in order to be satisfied by them as an accurate record on which judgement could be based. Another reported cause was that the delay occurred because of disagreement between the high court judge and his two assessors. The judge reached a guilty verdict but his assessors disagreed. In the high court, all matters of fact must be decided by a majority. *News Africa* (London), 31 August 2004, p. 7.

4. Tsitsi Dangarembga, *Nervous Conditions*, Harare: Zimbabwe Publishing House, 1988. This book, about the 'nervous conditions' of its female protagonists, such as anorexia and bulimia, was hailed internationally as a feminist statement in a hitherto male world of Zimbabwean writing. See Ann Elizabeth Willey and Jeanette Treiber, *Emerging Perspectives on Tsitsi Dangarembga: Negotiating the Postcolonial*, Trenton: Africa World Press, 2002.

5. Dambudzo Marechera, *The House of Hunger*, Oxford: Heinemann, 1978. This book, published before independence, became the most famous – if also the most controversial – Zimbabwean book. It spawned a huge, not always very good, critical literature. The first major book on his work was Flora Veit-Wild and Anthony Chennells, *Emerging Perspectives on Dambudzo Marechera*, Trenton: Africa World Press, 1999. For my own comments on his work, see Stephen Chan, *Composing Africa: Civil Society and its Discontents*, Tampere: Tampere Peace Research Institute, 2002, pp. 43-8.

6. For example, Brian Raftopoulos, *Beyond the House of Hunger*, Harare: Zimbabwe Institute of Development Studies, 1991; M.F.C. Bourdillon (Poor, *Harassed but Very Much Alive*, Gweru: Mambo Press, 1991) introduced his book on homeless Zimbabweans with the Marechera line: 'Trees too tired to carry the burden/Of leaf and bud, of bird and bough.'

7. Grant Lilford, 'Traces of Tradition', in Veit-Wild and Chennells, op. cit., p. 291.

8. Terence Ranger, *Peasant Consciousness and Guerilla War in Zimbabwe*, London: James Currey, 1985; David Lan, *Guns and Rain*, London: James Currey, 1985.

AIDS & Aid: Disease & Conditionality

The HIV infection rate in Zimbabwe has long been high. The sudden decline in living standards since 2000 has brought with it lower nutrition levels and even lower immunity to the various infections to which an HIV-sufferer is exposed. The number of deaths from AIDS, as a result, has soared – although, even now, causes of death are often listed in terms of the infection that was made possible by suppressed immune systems. Deaths officially by tuberculosis or malaria do not disguise the widespread but whispered knowledge that HIV/AIDS is rampant.

As long ago as 1997, Zimbabwe was top of 44 measured African countries in terms of HIV/AIDS prevalence.[1] Little was done in terms of mobilised government thinking at that time, or in the years that followed (other than a longstanding campaign testing donated blood for HIV). This contrasted markedly with what other African countries – although often belatedly – were doing or beginning to do.[2] Zimbabwe's top ranking in the HIV/AIDS prevalence table has now been taken over by South Africa, with Botswana also vying for what is a very dubious distinction. But both countries have the resource base to address the pandemic and, at last, both countries are moving in the direction both of mass education and the provision of generic antiretrovirals. Even in Zambia, antiretrovirals are available freely in the military. In Zimbabwe, generic antiretrovirals can now be manufactured and made available – but, as with all medicine from clinics and hospitals in today's Zimbabwe, the patient must pay for them and the price is beyond most sufferers in the stricken economy. Even with the manufacture of generics, Zimbabwean society still seems to exhibit a marked reluctance to discuss the subject of infection openly and freely. Mind you, when other free discussion is censored and restricted, the conditions for open debate – and debate without insults or condescension – about HIV/AIDS is also going to be limited. An oppositional and opportunistic culture has arisen in Zimbabwean discourse: the other side is always wrong, and the winning side had better grab what it can and glory in it. A trip to a Harare night-club in 2004 will see revellers sneeringly referring to thinner people as those 'who must be on antiret-rovirals', people somehow strong enough to be the dancing dead, while all and sundry seek new partners for the evening's entertainment. Only in 2004 has President Mugabe made some contribution to the HIV/AIDS awareness campaign. President Kaunda in Zambia did so fifteen years ago. I asked Morgan Tsvangirai therefore of his first awareness of the pandemic.

It was when I went to England in 1986, I was in Nottingham doing a diploma course. And that's when I got the first impact of HIV/AIDS in Europe [the British Government was sponsoring a huge television advertising campaign at that time]. But, back here in Zimbabwe then, people were ignorant. I mean, they were talking. There is this new disease called AIDS. Your hair goes old. You become thin – and all that. At that time I think we had not accepted the reality. Of course there was very little knowledge here about it. Mugabe went into denial. Because, really, he went on this denial crusade in a vicious way – 'there is no AIDS in Zimbabwe' – and yet I think the first cases were in fact around '85 or '86. And we did not take the political leadership necessary.

I mean, we always did have the highest infection rate. South Africa then followed later. I mean, they have made their own political blunders, and the argument backwards and forwards down there was very critical. I think what we lacked here was public awareness, public acceptance, political leadership over how to deal with this epidemic. It was very unfortunate. I know, in the ZCTU, when I was in the trade union movement, we started a programme that was in HIV/AIDS training, way back in the 1990s – '97, '98 – and we did a lot of programmes amongst the workers. Which, if that sort of leadership had been displayed at national level, I am sure that this country would have done a lot to lead in awareness programmes, in behavioural change, as well as some of the practices that have actu-ally increased the disease rather than control it.

I asked how Morgan Tsvangirai intended to lead a country into a pro-ductive future if a very great number of the people, and the productive workforce, had been afflicted by this disease.

That's why I told you about '98 when we started an AIDS pro-gramme. Because what we were saying was that, if this disease is going to hit your most productive assets, your human resource base is going to be decimated. That's your 15-49 age group. And I think part of the contribution to the lower population growth in this coun-try is as a result of the AIDS pandemic.

I remarked that there was a question here, not only of controlling a disease, but of a social philosophy of international relations. How do you deal, I asked, with the international agencies, the unofficial agencies, NGOs, who have made the pandemic into an 'AIDS industry' – of which they are in control – and who pretty much dictate how a country should go about responding to this health crisis?

Well, I think the response, the national response, to this kind of crisis should be defined by the nationals themselves. Cultures are different. Practices are different. In the absence of a treatment it is more of a cultural approach than an epidemiological one. So, I believe that, just like Uganda took a particular leadership because of their particular cultural practices,[3] I am sure that Zimbabwe should be able to define some of our own cultures that contribute to the expansion of infection. Things like infidelity, things like sex education at school, things like polygamy. Although here there's a problem. It's not polygamy as such but, if your brother dies, then by custom you can inherit the wife. That has contributed a lot to the spread. Debate around monogamy, abstinence, all these issues are important, have to be part of the national leadership focus. Once you have got that clearly, you can then mobilise the whole nation around that national agenda. We don't want to be like Botswana. Because many Batswana don't regard infidelity as anything unusual.[4]

So we have many kinds of particular national characteristics that must be taken into consideration if we have to confront this disease. Now, you ask me about what defined agendas by multilateral organisations come with this AIDS industry, with NGOs. I think there should just be a starting point – that we cannot accept defined programmes by outsiders. We should define something which is relevant to us and which we believe is going to lead to the resolution of this health crisis.

I said that this led us into a much broader question about overseas aid and assistance – about the entire question of international agendas forcing their way onto the national agenda.

It is indeed almost like an industry. I think at some point what is important, even for these multilateral organisations, is for the nation to define its own priorities. Clearly define its priorities to find a solution to the national crisis we face. If we were to have a choice between unemployment, and HIV/AIDS, as to which was the priority, I think that one would have to say that HIV/AIDS is the priority, and we need to put as much effort on it as we can put on other long-term developmental issues – because dead people can't develop.

They don't, I said, although sometimes they tend to vote. (Both laugh.) But, I asked, what about the aid industry in general? What about conditionality? How do you negotiate this? I asked what kind of negotiating philosophy an MDC government might adopt.

Well, I have said that if we want to be a government our philosophy would be based upon defining our own priorities and going to our international partners with a defined menu of priorities. You can be caught by international aid. I realised this when Zimbabwe became independent. It actually became dependent, you know, dependent rather than independent. For fifteen years the Smith regime – let's forget about the horror of it all for a minute – there was not a single item of foreign aid to this country. Yet, during that period, the country was able to diversify, was able to industrialise, was able to develop – although only in the minority sense. But the infrastructure was laid, not because of aid but because of the ingenuity, the entrepreneurship, that was demonstrated and developed during that period. But what I am trying to say is that, for a philosophy, that was proof. Aid dependence can be a hindrance. If not properly focused, aid can actually damage.

I mentioned that, earlier, we had been talking about globalisation. How, I asked, can you be part of globalisation without becoming a junior partner?

I know it's hard. My point is that we have hidden behind conditionality – which is meant to guarantee liquidity flows – because of our own lack of policy options. I think we should define our own priorities and policy options. These multilateral organisations must be engaged on our own priorities and negotiate on what we want – we having defined in our own minds what are clearly our priorities.

All easier said than done, I countered. But, as an example of the best that negotiation can do, I asked Tsvangirai about the work of finance minister Bernard Chidzero in the late 1980s and early 1990s. Chidzero had held the country's economic reins at about the same period that Tsvangirai was cutting his teeth as ZCTU leader.

Well, I think Bernard Chidzero was a very international expert. He lived within the [international] institutions, so he knew the politics of the institutions. However, Bernard Chidzero could not fully convince his colleagues in ZANU(PF) who had this insatiable demand to spend without investing in the people, without investing in expansion, without expanding the cake. They only wanted to eat what was there. And of course it was a very difficult situation, because he had to continue borrowing in order to satisfy this desire to spend without investing in the future. So I think, in the end, he became a victim. But as far as negotiating for the government, he was very, very good.[5]

I thought I should throw caution to the winds at this stage and mention the merits of a member of today's ZANU(PF). I said that, perhaps, Simba Makoni could do today what Bernard Chidzero did more than a decade ago.

> *Simba Makoni is not an economist. But I think he does have international respect and I think he would have used his international respect to leverage some of these negotiations. I think he does have leverage.*

I decided to extend the provocation. I mentioned that, two years ago, I had enjoyed a conversation with officials at the US Embassy, the persons concerned have now ended their tour in Zimbabwe, and their 'dream team' for Zimbabwe was Tsvangirai as president, with Simba Makoni as vice president.

> *But look, quite apart from my own personal relations – we are personally very good friends – I would have worked with him. We would have worked as a team. I would have felt no problem working with Simba Makoni, not because we agree, not because we are the same. First of all we are the same age (laughs)… but really, we approach issues from the same perspective. In our discussions we agree what is wrong and what needs to be done. So, what a beauty would that be?*

> *As for the American 'dream team' (laughs)… well, I certainly believe he has played, and I think he still can play a very important role in the political development of this country.*

I thought I would get to the point I was circling around. I said that, in our earlier discussions, I had asked about the lack of heavyweights in the MDC front bench. I said that, apart from people like Makoni, there weren't many who had the stature to undertake hands-on negotiations with incredibly sophisticated and very powerful negotiators from other governments, from the international financial institutions, the World Trade Organisation. I said that David needs all the stature he can get when going up against today's Goliaths, and there are many Goliaths.[6]

> *Yes, but I really think that you can imagine that Zimbabwe is in fact so well endowed with expertise. Do we have the capacity to identify such people? Yes. Do we have the will to bring such people on board? Yes, we do. And I am sure that any MDC government will have to get them on board.* [Here, Tsvangirai listed several names, some now working in international institutions. I have not reproduced those names here. I was not sure whether Tsvangirai listed them simply as possible recruits to an MDC government, or whether they were already sympathetic to the idea of an MDC

government.] *You have got, as you said, your Simba Makonis, and you have got some of the former UN employees who are here and who you can resort to, apart from the experience within the business community. I think that any government that does not see its human resource base as an asset to the whole country and is just focused on political issues is being paranoid about political correctness (laughs), and not focused on economic issues. One has to face this wide variety of skills that are available to the country.*

I remarked that a number of MDC members, perhaps hoping for senior positions in an MDC government, might think Tsvangirai was being far too generous to others.

I am sure people will understand. What we are trying to do is to find solutions to the myriad of problems that are not necessarily within the purview of political correctness. (Laughs.) I would certainly expand beyond just the narrow political defines.

Tsvangirai had been saying some open and radical things, so I thought we should wind up the conversation about international aid with a question about NEPAD (the so-called New Partnership for Africa's Development). If there was anything freighted with conditionality it was NEPAD. You get economic assistance if you're democratic. The MDC wants democracy but is against conditionality, so is the MDC for NEPAD?

No. No, I have not endorsed NEPAD, but I have endorsed good governance. You don't need anyone to define to you that you need to observe human rights. You need democratic principles and values for your own sake. You cannot institute these values on the basis of conditions that are being applied from outside. Africa needs democracy because democracy is good for Africa. And I don't believe that you need to negotiate good governance principles on the basis that it is the only way in which you receive aid. Democracy does not have a beggar mentality. It's unacceptable. It is a rider-and-horse attitude and I don't think Africa should have itself as the horse. And Africa cannot operate on the minimum denominator – just enough democracy to get enough aid. Democracy is a universal value. Maybe with national characteristics, but always observing human rights, respecting individual initiative, rewarding it, creating opportunities for everyone, and pulling your people out of poverty and subsistence and disease. That's something that Africa should stand up for. We don't need the West to define what's good for us. We can define it. We can define what's good for us.

Democracy not on the terms of others – in a way Tsvangirai was closer to some of the pan-Africanist intellectuals than he might have thought.

We would explore that in our next conversation.

The last conversation had been extremely interesting. It revealed exactly what Tsvangirai meant when he had talked earlier about inclusiveness. He would include people like Simba Makoni in an MDC government, and indeed anyone who could contribute to the political and economic regeneration of the country. He is against 'political correctness', by which he means the limitations of party labels. Even so, there are reasons why people choose to join, or remain within, a political party; and the sense of a nationalism may well be why someone like Makoni chooses to remain with ZANU(PF). Here, however, Tsvangirai had been talking about an independent process of nation-building. The West was not going to dictate to Zimbabwe – neither Western NGOs on the HIV/AIDS epidemic, nor the World Bank and IMF on conditions for liquidity flow, nor Western governments on NEPAD. For Tsvangirai, an independent nationalism was a modernised one – inclusive of all who could help in the modern technological terms that were now needed – but it came without the historical baggage of ZANU(PF). Whether this would be enough for ZANU(PF) figures to embrace is another question. And whether the MDC at large would, as freely as Tsvangirai, wish to be inclusive of others is very much an open question. If it happens then, ironically, Ibbo Mandaza's fantasy of a 'third force' might no longer appear fantastic.

Tsvangirai's views of the HIV/AIDS issue were of great interest. He never once talked of antiretrovirals but, instead, concentrated on the cultural conditions of prevention and control. I wanted very much to probe Tsvangirai on exactly what these cultural conditions entailed. Could there, after all, be an African democracy that arose from something accepted as African culture? Could there be an 'African' justice? Just as he was opening up in his conversation, a welter of further explorations also began to appear as necessary in order to understand his thinking.

Notes

1. For a discussion of that UNAIDS measure, see Nana Poku, *Regionalization and Security in Southern Africa*, Houndmills: Palgrave Macmillan, 2001, pp. 125-31.

2. For a view of this, with case examples particularly from Uganda and Botswana, see the special issue of *International Relations* (Guest editor; Nana K. Poku), XV:6, 2001.

3. The Uganda case example is in many ways a model. It did indeed engage in quiet debate and persuasion of cultural and religious groups – such as the Catholic Church – and established, again by patient discussion and negotiation, a modus operandi between government and international agencies and NGOs. Practices were codified and written, and based on prevalence rates; but there was also much unwritten that simply became good practice. See Justin O. Parkhurst, 'The Crisis

of AIDS and the Politics of Response: The Case of Uganda', in the special issue, ibid. It should be noted that Uganda has not conquered the disease. It has taken measurable steps to control it. This pandemic necessarily means a long-term, patient and, above all, kind, approach.

4. This is not particularly fair to the national effort in Botswana against HIV/AIDS. As early as 1993, a Presidential directive established the first government campaign against HIV/AIDS, and government policy now encompasses exactly those public education and awareness measures described as desirable by Tsvangirai. See Bertha Osei-Hwedie and Kwaku Osei-Hwedie, 'The Social Context of HIV/AIDS Policy in Africa', in Kemp Ronald Hope Sr (ed.), *AIDS and Development in Africa: A Social Science Perspective*, New York: Haworth Press, 1999. There have now been two medium-term plans to combat HIV/AIDS in Botswana, both officially launched and co-ordinated by the Ministry of Health. There is a Ministry of Health national policy document on HIV/AIDS, published in 1998, the same year that Tsvangirai recalls the ZCTU campaign. And free health care, including for HIV-infection, based on the distribution of geographically accessible clinics, was part of the 1997-2003 Eighth National Development Plan.

5. Chidzero was probably the most successful of all Zimbabwean finance ministers, particularly – as Tsvangirai says – in negotiating with the international financial agencies. Not all reviews of his work were flattering however. Christopher Gregory, 'Zimbabwe's Second Decade: Little Room for Manoeuvre?', in Larry Benjamin and Christopher Gregory (eds), *Southern Africa at the Crossroads?*, Rivonia: Justified Press, 1992, attacks Chidzero for not doing as much in free market reform as Gregory and other orthodox thinkers considered desirable. Chidzero had to steer a middle path between local expectations and international pressures. Contrary to Tsvangirai's view, Jeffrey Herbst, in *State Politics in Zimbabwe*, Berkeley: University of California Press, 1990, p. 134, shared Andrew Meldrum's conclusion that Chidzero seemed to have 'the firm backing of Mugabe and ZANU to thoroughly re-make Zimbabwe's economy' – Meldrum writing for Africa Report, May-June 1989, p. 40. It is clear that things did slip with Chidzero's ill-health and departure from the scene but, certainly, at the time of 1991, Chidzero had impressed sufficient states in the global community to be a serious candidate for the UN Secretary-Generalship.

6. This repeats a lament made as early as 1979 by Julius Nyerere, when he compared the state of third world negotiators going up against 'highly experienced people, armed with all the preparatory material done by sophisticated domestic and OECD staffs and their computers'. Julius K. Nyerere, *Unity for a New Order*, Dar es Salaam: Government Printer, 1979, p. 11. The third world negotiators are a little better now, but the first world negotiators are a lot better.

Traditional Culture, Modernity & Democracy

The paragon, the darling, of the Africa-essentialist left is the Tanzanian academic Issa G. Shivji. His use of Marxist vocabulary and analysis is such that his vision of an Africa, uninfected by Western, bourgeois, and imperialist influences, is itself infected by European socialist influences. Moreover, his emphasis on peasant mobilisation is drawn from a Chinese Maoist influence – so that the 'purely' and authentically African nature of Shivji's ideal state has nothing to do with historical culture as such, but everything to do with what the masses, particularly the rural, village-based peasant masses might seek to create as they move into a revolutionary phase. It is an irrepressibly romantic vision. It suffers in cases such as Zambia, where more of the population is urbanised than rural; and even in Zimbabwe after the land seizures and redistribution, where there will shortly survive many more commercial farmers and their workers than peasants. Even so, the impulse behind Shivji's work is immaculate. If Africa can somehow rid itself of the legacy that colonialism has brought, and renegotiate to Africa's advantage all the international links that are now imperialised, then the continent could start again. It is also a highly moral work, since the emphasis on peasants leading the fresh start is necessarily against the present corrupt ruling classes who benefit from the developing economies that the West needs for its own international purposes. But it is an archaic outlook for, without development, what Shivji really proposes is a pastoral Africa where, somehow, there will also be a Westminster-free democracy. ZANU(PF) intellectuals have been selective in appropriating parts of this vision. They would themselves inhabit what Shivji calls a 'developmentalist' state, but the peasants would somehow grow enough food, happily and democratically enough, to feed them in the city universities. They would endorse the seizing of land without knowing the complexities required to farm it. They would reject the imperialism of the West while benefiting from its grants and leisure technologies. They would repudiate Western democracy but insist that, one day, an African democracy will allow the peasants to make the decisions. In the meantime, they will do that within a vanguard party. Even Shivji is not so idealistic he would endorse the ransacking of his ideas by people who ransack more widely.

What, however, is Shivji's idea of an African democracy? He is, as noted above, committed to the belief that there will be a rural revolutionary phase, what he calls 'the battleground of the countryside'.[1] One can almost see ZANU(PF) theoreticians abstracting that into their justifications for the land seizures. Shivji, however, is also committed to the safeguarding of human rights. These are not suspended in the mass struggle forward. But his instruments of democracy are tame and insipid. They follow on from his concept that democracy should cascade upwards. However, it does this from the base of 'village assemblies' forming 'electoral colleges'.[2] By the time each electoral college has elected the next one above it, and the process culminates in the election of the president – or even, as in post-Tito Yugoslavia, a collective presidency[3] – the village peasant will have been left several cascades behind.

I do not mean to belittle Shivji's work. So many people have written critically, not so much of the Western democratic model, as the fact that it was imposed. Very few have tried to devise an alternative model. Whatever model emerges as 'African' will have to be, all critics agree, constitutionalised. Here again, there are very few drafts of what such a constitution might look like. Finally, at this stage anyway, the pan-Africanist search for an essentially 'African' form of democracy has been rhetorical and abstract. Tsvangirai knows this, but he rejects also the imposition of artifices such as NEPAD, and the assumption that only the Western model will measurably suffice in the international politics of today.

We cannot have a pastoral democracy. I think Africa has to skip some of the stages of the developmental path because of the advances that have been made, the exposures to technologies. Africans have even been exposed to new methods of social life. You cannot avoid those. However, I don't think that human rights, or democracy, can be defined in terms of African contexts – or any particular contexts. I think these are universal concepts.

You know, talking of Tanzanians, the Tanzanian president last night was talking about Zimbabwe being allowed to have its own democratic evolution. I said to someone I was talking to just this morning, 'My goodness, how can you have evolution, democratic evolution, when people are still using violence, repression? What kind of evolution is that?' I thought that man must not be allowed to get away with it. And I was talking to my press officers that he must not be allowed to get away with it. If it is endorsement of what Mugabe is doing, that is not democratic evolution. Because, after 24 years of independence, Zimbabwe should have consolidated all its democratic institutions and values. What evolution is he talking about? Way back to the Stone Age, where people are being beaten and burned in their own villages? So I said, 'well, this is solidarity of the leaderships and not solidarity with the people'.

Yes, and the intellectuals, who have this backward view about how to organise society, never leave their ivory towers. They don't even know what is happening in Chiredzi, what is happening in Binga. They are quite out of touch with reality.

I asked Tsvangirai whether we could develop the conversation towards an emerging, more concrete model of government – one that at least had pretensions to democracy, or at least some carefully limited democratic processes. I said that, with the dominance of the ANC in South Africa, that country had become to all intents and purposes a dominant-party state. It is not a single-party state, and no one in the ANC seriously proposes that, fifteen years after the fall of Kaunda in Zambia, there should be a reprise of the one-party state idea in Africa. Particularly if the opposition is ineffective and in a distinct minority, the ANC can run a dominant-party state and simultaneously claim it is democratic and doing everything NEPAD says it should do. There is a version of this in Egypt. The most successful international model of a dominant-party state is Singapore. There, two opposition MPs sit in parliament, they speak their minds, no one listens, and Lee Kwan Yew creates a dynasty – a republican perpetual First Family within a dominant-party state. No one is saying that there will be a son-of-Mugabe as president in the future, but some ZANU(PF) strategists are attracted to the idea of a dominant-party state; they will be able to rule quite freely, provided they accord some small space and some nicety towards a limited opposition – have the best of both worlds and not even have to pretend to be 'African'.

Lee Kwan Yew, yes, he was ruling a city-state. Unfortunately, you can't reform ZANU(PF). They are dominating not by the will of anybody, but by brute force.

I mentioned that the Singaporeans were not always very soft in their politics.

No, I'm not saying that. And, anyway, if ZANU(PF) wants to model itself on a dominant-party state, then they've left it too late. They have left it to the point where their credibility is being ques-tioned by the rest of society. The reason why Lee Kwan Yew was able to dominate was that he was able to deliver economically, and socially, to the extent that politics was subsumed by economic per-formance, right?[4] In our case, the reason why our politics is upside down in terms of the Singaporean model is because 80 per cent of the people are poor. And you cannot continue to appeal for patriotic commitment to ZANU(PF) while a few elites are benefiting and the rest of society is poor. You cannot do that. They should really have tried the dominant-party trick a long time ago.

I speculated what Tsvangirai, if he indeed became president of Zimbabwe, would say to his colleague presidents in the African Union – not all of whom are particularly democratic.

Well, I was grappling with this just the other day. The question of just how do you have a go at this club of dictators? And how do you hope to influence it? Do you stay out of it? Do you go in and make your vast contribution? (Laughs.) At the expense of being considered a square peg in a round hole? (Still laughing.)

I rather ruefully recalled, having advised the newly-independent state of Eritrea, how its President Isaias Aferwerki had at his first speech to what was then still the OAU really lectured the other Presidents about democracy. They were all astounded. But now he too has become dictatorial, and my friends who were heroes in their liberation struggle are in prison without charge or trial.

A dictator himself. A warning. Well, my approach is that Zimbabwe is an African state. The only way in which you can have an influence is when you become a success. You become a success when you are seen to be moving positively towards economic growth, when you are putting democratic institutions into place, when you are avoiding the pitfalls and tendencies towards repression and monopoly politics. When you are expanding rather than narrowing the democratic space.

Botswana is a big country with a small population, but it has become a model because it has become successful. I believe that the path of economic prudence...

I interjected that now he was sounding just like Gordon Brown, the British Chancellor of the Exchequer, who was always going on about economic prudence. (Both laugh.)

You know we need to do that – be economically prudent. I mean, they may be words, but I think that they express what we need to be a successful state. In all its dimensions. But, as far as lecturing to other African states – well, they just tend to be negative. I got a lot of negative reaction.

But at some point in time we will have to stand up and take principled steps – without necessarily lecturing people. The problem that we have with some of these African states is that they connive, they apologise for each other – like the Tanzanian President for Mugabe. Such an attitude is not helpful. It doesn't provide credibility for

Africa, it undermines trust in African leadership. The elite simply cannot try to protect itself from the rest of the population.

I asked about the 'rest of the population', which in many African states can be very diverse. What about leadership and ethnic violence in Africa?

First and foremost we have to start off with the basis that in diversity there is strength. In Zimbabwe we have our own various ethnic groups, groups with different cultures, different races. I think, as MDC, we have provided the leadership for uniting the people, regardless of the diversity, uniting the people around one agenda as one nation, but accepting that actually with this diversity Zimbabwe could have been a much stronger nation than it has been. The massacres in Matabeleland have inspired this blatant resentment from that region. The only organisation that has rallied people around one national agenda is the MDC. It has gone beyond the traditional divisions of ethnicity, racism and all that. It's difficult, but I think not impossible, to unite people around national interest, a national agenda – for everyone to benefit. Not just one narrow ethnic group to benefit.

I said that some have indeed found it almost impossible. What about, I asked, the slaughter of Tutsis by Hutus in Rwanda?

That was a tragic international omission. Whether they call it commission or omission is, to me, irrelevant. It is something that should not have been allowed. I think the first thing is that some sort of healing process has to be instituted. You need structures, you need policies, you need programmes...

I asked, and do you need laws?

Laws, of course. That's part of it. I don't believe that you can have Truth and Reconciliation processes. I think what is needed is Truth and Justice. Because there's the problem of repeating it, opportunities of repeating it – if it is not nabbed and some finality is put to it. Otherwise history will repeat itself. So I think justice. People must not be allowed to get away with injustice. Because here you have to deal with the cries of the victims. At the same time you have also to deal with the perpetrators.

I asked in what way law and justice could be enforced. In the same case of Rwanda, where so many people were involved in committing slaughter – and the formal courts and tribunals can't cope – it seems that they may be tried before traditional village or community 'courts'. But this raises questions of equity and transparency.

To me, I thought it was an innovation which is worth looking at, and I'll tell you why. In a traditional rural community, if some-

body burned someone else's house, there are penalties that are his-torical within that society, within that community. If someone raped someone else's wife, if somebody raped someone's child, if somebody killed someone, there were always ways in which local traditional African communities dealt with it. Now, the problem is indeed to do with the competence of the legal framework in which those courts operate, and the competences within those courts. It's one which is open to abuse, and that's what you need to guard against. But, to me, I thought it was an innovation – giving instant justice within those communities. Also contributing to the fact that the communities actually own the justice system was an innovation worth looking at.

I was not entirely easy with this – although Tsvangirai had merely said it was an innovation worth looking at. But it raised the spectre of 'tra-ditional' Truth and Justice committees. It raised the spectre of venge-ance being given local licence, rather than any truth or justice. It also sounded very like Shivji's idea of community ownership of processes that somehow cascaded upwards. I mentioned that in Libya there had been, within a revolutionary society, a system of autonomous local dis-tricts and committees, but this created problems as to whether local or central government had the last word – and, if it were central, then autonomous local ownership was lost.[5] In the early radical years of Jerry Rawlings' Ghana, local revolutionary committees had much power, but they simply could not deal with the complex issues of modern develop-ment and regeneration,[6] not to mention justice.

All that needs to be looked at. There must be provision for appeals systems from the sort of local courts we talked about. The appeal structure must be clear.

I said that what Tsvangirai was talking about was a mix of the tradi-tional and modern, and the modern would be located in the appeals structure. But Tsvangirai had portrayed himself in our earlier discus-sions as the great moderniser.

Mixing traditional and modern. It's a good question that one has to confront. The choice is the extent to which you can continue to sus-tain the traditional institutions without necessarily being in conflict with modern institutions, and without undermining your own cul-ture. How far can you take your culture? Is there a conflict between culture and modernity? There are some things that I do think we need a complete break with. I think there will be a need to have discussions. Debate as to what we take along and what we discard. Because I believe there are certain institutional practices in the traditional system that are archaic to modern thought and modern development. But some things are of great value. The Japanese still

75

Shinto shrines, but that does not make the Japanese backward. ...ple still go to Buddha, but that doesn't mean they are not mod- ..., it does not mean they have cut themselves off from modern ...cans.

I saw that Tsvangirai was not intending literally to establish local systems of judgement without modern safeguards, but the concept of a mixed culture – traditional and modern – clearly appealed to him. I said he would need not only a brilliant minister of finance in his government, and a brilliant minister of justice, but a brilliant minister of culture as well.

Certainly. Because we have to walk a very thin dividing line of choice. There are pulling forces. There will be pulling forces for more tradition in order to reinforce our identity – but there will be even stronger forces, because of levels of education, the impact of urbanisation and globalisation on the people, that will pull on the other side. I think the balance is one that is going to be very difficult to make. But it is necessary to make those choices.

I commented that there is a lot that has begun to be written about Zimbabwean history, culture and tradition, but it was not yet fully developed. I said that this was one of those rare sites in Africa where great stone cities and buildings were constructed, and the chain of them clearly suggested a complex trading and transport route leading to the sea and perhaps even international markets.

Yes, we need more work on that. In order to link our past to ourselves we need more people who have to examine where we have come from, where we are, because that will help define our future. We have a great history in this country, going back thousands of years.[7] It's a rich culture – especially the Shona culture, the Shona tradition.[8] But it needs a lot of archaeological debate and modern historical method – historians to analyse our culture, background, where there have been ruptures in this whole journey, where we need to connect.

I asked whether it was only a matter of culture that could be appreciated in the remains of stone cities. I said that I had dined with the author Charles Mungoshi the other night and we had enjoyed a fascinating discussion about how different languages have different tenses. In Finnish, for instance, there seem to be seven different versions of the future conditional. And Mungoshi was talking about the many different tenses there are in Shona, compared to the few in most European languages. Complex tense variables tend to mean a more complex sense of time. It seemed to me that this sort of linguistic investigation had not really been undertaken. The great Ghanaian philosopher, Kwame

Gyekye, has written – almost as a riposte to all those black American professors who teach Afro or Africana Studies without any knowledge of African languages – that African philosophy should start where it 'should have started', and that is with the linguistic foundations.[9]

> *If you go to the various Shona dialects then Mungoshi is right. We need more scholarly work on this. We need people to analyse this. Because I think colonialism sort of made a break, which had a very serious impact on the language, culture and views, so I do think we need to re-contact.*

We had at this stage some light banter about university professors, how George Kahari was really one of only a handful of distinguished figures at the University of Zimbabwe writing about Shona language, how certain politicians – the minister of education, Aeneas Chigwedere, being an example – would be much better off pursuing lives of scholarship. 'He is one of the great scholarly workers on Africa,' said Tsvangirai, who all the same didn't rate his skills as a politician. 'He's a real scatterbrain.' I said I knew all about absent-minded professors, having the misfortune to be one. But these two individuals were not MDC members, so the entire question of MDC intellectual depth in key areas was raised again. And, of course, there was a burning political issue at stake in today's Zimbabwe. It had defined all political development since 2000. That was the land issue. It's not just a question of economics, I said, or even Zvobgo's agrarian enterprise, but it was, in ZANU(PF) terms, the key traditional foundation to modern nationalism.

> *Yes. It's a complex issue which needs unpacking. All these subterranean meanings and you need to unpack them. Again, tradition and land. It's a very emotional nationalistic combination. It's the whole basis of African existence in the traditional sense. Now, when you take the land in the economic and modern sense, it assumes a different meaning. Land means jobs. It means health, it means education, it means all the economic facets that make life improved. Right? So mixing the traditional meaning of land and the modern meaning of land, that it is an economic asset rather than an emotional asset, it becomes complex really.*

I asked how he could unpack it. The entire ZANU(PF) discourse had traded off this very strongly indeed. The emotional content may now be too strong.

> *Yes, ZANU(PF) has. But I think one thing I can say is that it is an irreversible process.*

I looked up from my note-taking, monitoring of the tape recorder. What's irreversible?

What they have done. It's irreversible. However, the methodology used to do it undermines, cuts across, the traditional and the modern meanings of land. Going back to the traditional meaning of land, it's actually a retrogressive step because you are going back to sub-sistence rather than moving forward with an emotion that fits modern times. The methodology should have taken into consideration the modern meaning of what land ownership and land tenure is all about. There is the whole question also of equity. But, you know, when you start bringing in the modern meaning of land as an economic asset, it actually undermines the role of tradition, the role of traditional chiefs – because, if I had a farm, and I am given title to it, the tenure system already undermines my traditional relationships. So the land distribution is really neither traditional nor modern. I think it's a complex issue and we need to move away from just emotion. Of course you can have whole communal areas that can still retain some of the traditional aspects of land, but you have a modern sector which should take on a much more modern and thriving role – because the country has to go forward.

And no. I wouldn't want to go for state farms. In our Restart policy documents we said that 'the land policy will be based on need and not greed', and that's neither state greed nor individual greed. Capitalist forms of ownership are always based on greed. It's a driving force. But you also need equity. You need a balance. We will actually be a hybrid – that, you need.

Also land is not just about agriculture. It has all to do with environment. All the environmental issues now come in, conservation and all these other issues.

I smiled. Is that why you can't bear to cut down that tree?

(Laughs.) You can't. You can't cut down trees. You know the damage that has been done to the ecosystem in this country during the last three to five years? It's astronomical. We will have to reinstitute measures of conservation again. There's been destruction in the conservation areas, I mean the wild parts, in the natural areas which have been so world-renowned. And they've all been devastated by this lawlessness that has characterised the land reform programme – if it is land reform at all. The other fundamental issue is that we need to distinguish between land distribution and land reform. The concept being that land reform is a holistic approach. Don't look at just distributing a piece of land. It's not about just giving out pieces of land. It's about linking land to industrialisation, being holistic in the same way we make all development holistic – rather than just looking at distribution as a one-off satisfaction of dealing with a colonial issue. It is considered a colonial issue but,

to me, it is a challenge for the long-term, for the long-term develop-
ment of the country.

In some ways it was a great pity that the MDC did not make these
points about land at an earlier stage. The land seizures had taken it by
surprise just as it was enjoying its victory in the constitutional referendum in 2000. The sorts of distinction that Tsvangirai now made were
not made then. Nor are they yet made by ZANU(PF), and Tsvangirai's
description of government policy as a 'one-off satisfaction' could not
have been better put.

And the question of irreversibility – did that apply only to those
having had land seized not being able to reclaim it? What about those
who now owned land – not always poor peasants but often already rich
ZANU(PF) cadres who have used this nationalist device further to
enrich themselves? Was this corruption also irreversible? What would
a Tsvangirai government do in its Truth and Justice Commission about
unjust gains? And, if it did do something, how would this affect the
healing process that Tsvangirai also talked about? I wanted to explore
these questions in our next conversation.

In the meantime, what was remarkable about the conversation now
ending was the number of similarities between Tsvangirai's thinking
and that of many ZANU(PF) thinkers. Affinities with Simba Makoni
and admiration of Edison Zvobgo, belated recognition from the fiery
ZCTU campaigner against structural adjustment about how well Bernard Chidzero actually did – all these might not be the only markers
of similarity.

Tsvangirai's affection for the principle of local ownership, even of
judicial processes, linked him to the pastoral cascading-upwards model
of African democracy proposed by Shivji. His great commitment to
the value of tradition – even if ameliorated by his greater commitment
to modernisation – in effect recognised the uses of culture put forward by Ali Mazrui as summarised earlier. His rejection of NEPAD
did not mean his rejection of universal values, but the acceptance both
that universality could not be dictated, and that universality could have
many local twists. In many ways Tsvangirai could easily have been a
progressive member of a ZANU(PF) cabinet before 1997 and his dis-
illusionment with Mugabe. He had been a ZANU(PF) member and
an early admirer of Mugabe and, frankly, yes, the 'dominant-party
trick' was now too late for ZANU(PF), because it should really have
incorporated Tsvangirai in the mid-1990s. It would have had its dominant-party state then.

What clearly separates Tsvangirai from ZANU(PF) is moral vision.
The way ZANU(PF) has gone about land reform is, to him, simply
wrong. The ZANU(PF) approach to equity, democracy and transparency is simply wrong. The ZANU(PF) persecution of all those who

put mazrui + shivji in culture week

stand against it is simply wrong. For Tsvangirai, what is right is what is facilitating of freedom and a free mixed society. It would be even more right if that free mixed society could also be economically productive and socially progressive. In those broad but foundation principles it is hard to disagree with this Tsvangirai.

Notes

1. Issa G. Shivji, *Fight My Beloved Continent: New Democracy in Africa*, Harare: SAPES Books, 1992, p. 45.
2. Issa G. Shivji, 'State and Constitutionalism: A New Democratic Perspective', in Issa G. Shivji (ed.), *State and Constitutionalism: An African Debate on Democracy*, Harare: SAPES Books, 1991, p. 43.
3. Although I should really point out the abject failure of that collective presidency. See, among others, Ivo Goldstein, *Croatia: A History*, London: Hurst, 1999, Chapters 11-13; Sabrina P. Ramet, *Nationalism and Federation in Yugoslavia 1962–1991*, Bloomington: Indiana University Press, 1992, Part II; and for the failure of the collectivised state as a whole, both Yugoslavia as a state committed to collectivised production, and as a collectivity of different national and ethnic groups, see the succinct summary by Christopher Cviic, *Remaking the Balkans*, London: Pinter, 1991.
4. Here Tsvangirai is absolutely right. Tatu Vanhanen, *Prospects of Democracy: A Study of 172 Countries*, London: Routledge, 1997, p. 148, calculated that 'the degree of resource distribution is so high' in Singapore that the country is perfectly stable.
5. For one such,and rather amusing, case example see John Davis, *Libyan Politics: Tribe and Revolution*, London: I.B. Tauris, 1987, pp. 137-41.
6. For a consideration and debate on exactly the economic choices Ghana confronted, see Jeffrey Herbst, *The Politics of Reform in Ghana*, 1982–1991, Berkeley: University of California Press, 1993. For a short note on the problems the Workers Defence Committees and People's Defence Committees caused law and order, and civil society, see pp. 28-9.
7. Hundreds in any case, if the ruins of Great Zimbabwe are the measure of what Tsvangirai means. These date back to the 13th century.
8. Although Ndebele cultural historians might dispute the word 'especially'. Again, if Tsvangirai is locating culture within the Great Zimbabwe epoch, it is well to remember that the remains of stone cities stretch across modern Zimbabwe. The Khami Ruins are near Bulawayo. For a fascinating discussion of Ndebele culture, including nationalist political culture, near the Matopos Hills, see Terence Ranger, *Voices from the Rocks: Nature, Culture and History in the Matopos Hills of Zimbabwe*, Oxford: James Currey, 1999.
9. Kwame Gyekye, *An Essay on African Philosophical Thought: The Akan Conceptual Scheme*, Cambridge: Cambridge University Press, 1987, p. 212.

Healing & the Future

The land 'reform' programme, with its 'one-off satisfaction', would leave Zimbabwe having to inherit many problems. Regaining agricultural productivity and halting ecological depredation are only two of them. Equity, however, will be the key issue. What was meant, crudely, to establish an equity in terms of racial ownerships of the land has become a series of inequities in terms of which black person now owns what. Many people now have a stake in not giving up what they have acquired, because what they have acquired – at no personal cost – is so attractive. How, I asked Morgan Tsvangirai, do you set about a process of national healing when people still retain what they have inequitably gained?

Well, I think unscrupulous gains are not equitable. What we need is a rationalisation process. We cannot allow people to have five farms whilst others don't even have a small plot of land.

I remarked that a certain well-known intellectual, an aficionado of Shivji's vision of peasant revolution and peasant ownership, is rumoured to have acquired four farms.

(Laughs.) Yes, yes indeed. But the question is: what rationalisation programme? There is a Land Commission trying to deal with the equity aspect and the legal aspect. But you cannot move to that stage unless you have done a national audit of what's there. This is where you establish whether Mr well-known so-and-so has four farms, or what. But you must understand we have to break the political patronage that was used by ZANU(PF) to distribute this national asset. We can't go back to pre-2000 but, at the same time, we are not going to endorse what ZANU(PF) has done.

Without in some way endorsing, or just accepting it, how will healing begin? I asked whether any other course would not simply inflame political difficulties.

No, the rationalisation programme will be equitable to the extent that those who have will have something which is equitable in rela-

tion to others – rather than 'what I have got cannot be touched'. We cannot have such a solution. After all, it's ZANU(PF) patronage to ZANU(PF) followers. What about the majority – who just happen to be MDC supporters? So again it needs to be thought through.

The rationalisation programme must be seen to be equitable, legal, transparent – so the land tenure system that is put in place is seen as transparent by everybody. Besides, we are not only talking about the new areas. We also have other neglected areas, the communal areas for instance. The small-scale farming areas where people have farms but they are not doing anything with them. That's why the audit is important because it will tell you who has to be there, how it is to be done, what kind of land tenure system, with what objective. Because I am sure that within a period, and I don't foresee this as a short-term issue – this is a five- to ten-year national programme, this is the kind of period I am looking at – it has to be slow, but it has to be final.

I noted that the agricultural consequences of land seizure and redistribution did not reveal any great agricultural thinking on ZANU(PF)'s part. What expertise will the MDC be able to draw upon for a long-term rationalisation programme?

We have already got people who are agricultural experts. And the Commission itself, with Professor Rukuni who has done the first Commission report, we believe that we can utilise that kind of expertise, we can bring it in. What is the feature of the ZANU(PF) methodology is that it is haphazard, it is unscientific, it is chaotic. What you need is to bring order and legality, a long-term tenural system, so that people can start investing and making productive use of the land again.

And I stress that the rationalisation programme is not a revenge programme. Even Mr Well-known So-and-so, even if he no longer has four farms, we are not revenging. We are putting in order a system which will create the healing you are talking about. Because there are so many people who have been excluded from the whole process. How do you justify that we are replacing a white minority elite with a black minority elite? The asset has to be equitably shared. Not equally shared, but equitably shared. And it has to be seen to be equitable.

I asked if we could talk about the future in other terms – in terms jointly of a future Zimbabwe and a future Morgan Tsvangirai. Let us, I said, imagine a future in which Tsvangirai has become President. He's had five years and he is up for re-election. What would you hope to say to the nation in terms of what you have accomplished, and what you still dream about for the future?

Well, I would be happy with a country which is at peace with itself. With opportunities for every child in the country. Inclusive, democratic, and that can realise its potential. Because the country has a huge potential, both in the medium and the long term, the potential of the people of Zimbabwe is enormous. Democratic, prosperous, and a country which is able to be recognised in Africa as one of the leading nations.

Recognised for all the positive reasons of what a progressive country should be. Stable, properly democratic and prosperous. I think Africa has not found a model state. (Laughs ruefully.) South Africa is attempting it, but is still young. They have not been tried and tested with the vagaries of development. Ten years is too short a period. Zimbabwe could have been a model state. Botswana is attempting to be a model state – but it can't be a typical state, such resources and such a small population. But Zimbabwe still can be. That's the sort of Zimbabwe I would like to see.

Let's dream, I said. Not vaingloriously, but let's dream. Suppose, I said, you did all this and after ten years as President you were nominated for the Nobel Peace Prize. What would you like the citation to read? You can be immodest, I said, it's obviously a dream – a nice dream.

A nice dream... yes.... Look, something like 'a man of very humble beginnings who has achieved so much for his own people, fought for democracy, established one of the most progressive, one of the most positive... no... managed to define a positive nature in Africa'.

You know, there is so much that is negative, there is too much pessimism. I would like to leave after ten years a country which is a proud beacon, one of the bright spots of Africa. I would like to see that. It would be a disappointment, I would feel I had betrayed, that I had been a failure if I did not achieve that.

I said that he had faced so much persecution and adversity. We had been talking for hour after hour and, at every opportunity, he still sounded like an idealist.

Well, I'm sure idealism is also a pathfinder to good things. It's a beacon in itself. It's a beacon along which you can travel. But yes, I think we must never be overcome, we must never allow all our obstacles – all the obstacles we face in life – to be a hindrance to progress. Not give in to obstacles, we have to find solutions. As far as I am concerned, life is about struggle and overcoming these obstacles.

Between August 2004 and March 2005, when the parliamentary elections are due, there will be almost eight months of obstacles. What work on himself, I asked, is Morgan Tsvangirai going through to prepare himself for these difficult months?

Yes, some months from now we go into the elections. I have focused myself on trying to fight for standards because I believe that, without those standards, the path to the election will be acrimonious, bloody and violent. So at every given platform I say to myself, 'we have to fight for an electoral framework which the people of Zimbabwe can have confidence in, because they have experienced brute force, violence, terror, at every turn of every election. We must have a difference this time round'.

I remarked that, recently, the government had announced a slight relaxation of the electoral rules.[1]

Cosmetic. We have to fight for even wider rules. That's why I'm saying that government has made a positive response, but it's insufficient to create the conditions that will build the necessary confidence in the people. So that is the first aspect. The other aspect is that we have to mobilise national and international opinion in order to achieve those standards. We are beginning to see a flexible response from SADC, from the African Union, from the United Nations, from the European Union, from the Americans, as far as the next elections are concerned. Why? Because everyone realises that without a free and fair election there will be no legitimate outcome in March. A legitimate outcome will be the basis for resolving the Zimbabwean crisis. So I am focusing on that.

The other thing is that I am also preparing myself and the MDC to take responsibility for the mandate which is going to come at that election. I am very confident that we will succeed, and so we must start putting in place – we must be prepared to govern – we must be putting in place promises, programme options, that an MDC administration can use after March to deal with the mess that has already been created. So I think preparing for that is really very important. We must not always be focusing on Mugabe and ZANU(PF). We must now deliver an image of what MDC is all about and what it is capable of delivering to the people of Zimbabwe.

I replied that, instead of behaving like an opposition, the MDC would be behaving like a government-in-waiting. But, even if the MDC wins, these are parliamentary elections. Tsvangirai would himself still be a President-in-waiting.

It will be the basis of moving towards the Presidential elections. And, yes, I know what you want to say... yes, we can discipline ourselves to behave like a government-in-waiting. I am very conscious of that. I realise there have been gaps, there were gaps in thinking in the long-term. We were just reacting. A lot of our people were reacting. We don't want this. But you see, putting forward long-term, well-thought-out solutions to the myriad of problems that we face is a tall order. And yes, I agree that having a shadow cabinet is all part of developing people's skills in government. Being in parliament has given us an opportunity to expose some of our key leaders to government institutions. And, from running cities, that was another big challenge to our people to learn the skills of governance. And they've been harassing us but, even so, it was still like throwing a child in the deep end.

I replied that Tsvangirai was saying that he and the MDC had learnt much in the last few years. I asked, if he was beginning all over again now, but with the wisdom of hindsight, what would he do differently?

I think, first and foremost, the constitutional debate would have been handled differently. We thought it was moving from an independence constitution to a democratic constitution, and that would require very skilful negotiations.

We should have been more thoughtful in our approach to Mugabe in negotiating the constitution than we were. It was a lost opportunity. We had sufficient power in the country to persuade Mugabe to negotiate. I think we should have urged him a bit, without necessarily having to go for everything.

He was saying something very fundamental at this point. You mean, I asked, you should have held out a small olive branch?

Yes. Yes. I think we should have done differently.

I remarked, a little taken aback at this stage, that such an approach would have required considerable discipline of the MDC's hotheads.

Yes. Yes. The party itself, because of its infancy and diverse skills... I think I would have done differently. We would have done differently if we had restructured the party in a way which was not conflictual. It is too radical. Sometimes it undermines confidence in it. I think I would have restructured the party to be more wide at the base of its representation. There are people in various roles I would have changed – because they have skills in other areas but they don't have skills in what was most needed.

It's a party which is diverse in its constituencies. But I think we moved too fast into a formalised party – because we were contesting elections.

I said there had been no choice if the elections were to be contested.

Yes, we had to contest. Yes. The idea was that we needed more mobilisation to confront the regime, put pressure on the regime – rather than become a party which became itself a target. I think internationally I would have changed the priorities. We should have invested more in Africa in our infancy than in Europe and the United States. They were quick to understand us, but not really to help us. We needed to build a solid base in Africa. So I would have put the African agenda more than the Western-oriented human rights thrust that we had.

I mean Sweden, for example, was swift to understand us and to help us. But, in Africa, opposition politics was always viewed as rebel politics, and it has taken a long time to convince people that we are a serious movement to consider, and that this is nothing to do with the West, it is everything to do with the social and political situation in Zimbabwe.

But you can't rewind the clock, I said. You have to go forward to March. But what will happen after March if you lose?

Well, obviously we will always plan for the worst and hope for the best. If we lose, that's not the end of the story. Struggle is not measured in terms of a time frame. It will be a lost opportunity, but it doesn't mean we shelve the struggle. The struggle has to continue. We will be a much more mature organisation. But I think we will have to handle, have to prepare to handle the outcome, the worst outcome, because otherwise it will seem like a devastated last hope. I know the enormity of the anxiety with which people look forward to this election.

I said that after the last loss, after the 2002 presidential elections, Tsvangirai had published what must be one of the most moving open political letters – not just in African political history, but it was something remarked upon internationally. This was the 'among you walk heroes' letter, and it was very much to address the devastation people felt. I asked point-blank, how much devastation can the MDC constituency take?

(Sighs.) I think the presidential election was so devastating for everybody. That's why, at this stage, the issue of do we go in under these conditions or should we just say, look, if this man is not prepared to give in, why should we go into a process which is already predetermined, and go and just cut our hope forever? It would have very serious fallout. I can even see a situation in which fragmentation may be possible. I can even foresee people thinking about some of the most outrageous options, that Mugabe has closed the democratic route, let's look for other undemocratic means to fight the system. There will be those temptations. I can foresee that.

That will be your young hotheads, I said.

Yes, but then it makes us, who are at the forefront of this democratic movement, irrelevant. If those kinds of options are put on the agenda then obviously we cannot be part of that.

Morgan Tsvangirai is neither Jerry Rawlings nor Thomas Sankara, I said.

I am not.

But what, I asked, if the hotheads were actually successful? What if they did a Jerry Rawlings? Undemocratic, but it brings change. What, I asked, would be his response to such a change under such conditions?

I will still think it will be the most unfortunate way of bringing democratic change to the country. It will be a reversal of the whole idea of our struggle. Instead of moving forward – because change of personalities for the sake of change is not transformation – it would be backwards. What we are talking about here is a complete political transformation, a new political paradigm in the country. Because, instead of moving towards instituting democratic culture, what Mugabe and ZANU(PF) have done is they have gone the other way. We need to bring ourselves back to the ideal that led us to fight for liberation in the first place.

I said that the idea that liberation had been betrayed had been expressed even by ZANU(PF) supporters. Even though Alexander Kanengoni might now write occasional journalism that is 'besmirched with narrow-mindedness', I still thought that his 1997 novel, *Echoing Silences*, stood as a great book at the close of the 20th century.[2] At the end of this book there is a spirit convention in heaven. People like Herbert Chitepo are addressing the rally. All of the old names on the new street signs in Harare are there, and they're saying that the revolution has in fact been betrayed, that the true values have been betrayed by the current regime. I said that it was a very brave thing for Kanengoni to have written at that time.

That I agree with you. I agree with you. Somebody was saying, 'where did the revolution lose its course?' (Laughs.) And that's where you have a revolution reduced to an 'agrarian racist enterprise'. A very, very, very fundamental statement.

I thought now was the time to ask him the big question. Would you go into retirement if you lost?

I… I pose myself the question. I always say to the people…

I interrupted him. I said, they might drop the charges, go light on you, your life could become normal again, you could be a normal family man…

I am sure that… I would have to find a new motivation. But I have to prepare myself to say, 'look, I think you need somebody else to take the struggle forward'. I know what people will say. 'Keep on fighting.' But, really, some of these processes need new blood – new challenges. And I will be part of the struggle but certainly not always at the head.

I had not expected him to say that. But I mustered myself and said his statement was a very elegiac, a sad, but natural place to end the conversation. I was in fact a little stunned by all he had said. He had opened himself both graciously and fully. He had taken quite a number of long hours out of his schedule to talk to me. I had, in time-honoured fashion, made a complete mess of his very tidy desk – tapes scattered over it as I had raced to replace one cassette after another; the transparent wrappings of the new cassettes littering its surface. He would be relieved, I was sure, to see the back of me. I turned the tape machine off and said 'Thank you'. Then he rose and asked me to walk with him in the beautiful garden.

Notes

1. This was in June 2004. The 26-member ZANU(PF) politiburo agreed there should be transparent ballot boxes and an independent election commission. The polls would be held all in one day, not two; the number of polling stations would be increased, and verification of ballots would take place at the polling stations. Tsvangirai was quoted as saying: 'The proposals meet some opposition demands, but fall far short of guaranteeing a free and fair poll.' The 'independent' election commission would have its head appointed by Mugabe and its members by parliament. And Mugabe himself hinted at the limits to electoral reform: 'We will not allow the erstwhile imperialists to judge our elections. We ask our friends to judge us.' This seemed to exclude US and European election observers. Whether 'our friends' would include Commonwealth observers is unclear, but would seem to leave room for African observation. Associated Press release, 30 June 2004.

2. Alexander Kanengoni, *Echoing Silences*, Harare: Baobab Books, 1997. For some of my comments praising this book, see Stephen Chan and Ranka Primorac, 'The Imagination of Land and the Reality of Seizure: Zimbabwe's Complex Reinventions', in *Columbia University Journal of International Affairs*, 57:2, 2004, pp. 73-4.

A Rueful Reflection

He wanted to show me around his garden, of which he was inordinately proud. The house, a sprawling single-floor bungalow, sits in the middle of it, but it is the garden that delighted Morgan Tsvangirai. 'When my wife and I first saw it,' he said, 'I thought, yes, this is it. This is it. I don't want to move anymore. This will do. This is it.' His street is far enough away from the main roads for the neighbourhood to have a countryside suburban feel. The only traffic sounds are the occasional returnings home of neighbours who then honk their horns so that their guards will open the gates. Not quite up-market enough to have electronic gates. Strathaven is not Borrowdale, the elite north-eastern suburb. But I had noticed, in downtown Harare, street hawkers selling electronic gate posts and intercoms – curiously without the wiring, so whether these were new South African goods smuggled across the border, or dug up from outside the gates of Borrowdale I didn't know. Or care. The luxuries of that suburb stand in too much contrast with the emerging underclass in Zimbabwe. It is emerging because, simply, it wasn't there before. This is not to say there was no poverty. There was a great deal of that. Before the mid-1990s, however, there had always been the aspiration to live a middle-class life and the sense that, if you worked hard or somehow got lucky, or both, then it was possible. A middle-class life, the lower reaches of it anyway, might be a small house in Chitungwiza – but the electricity would work, the television would not be stolen, the salary would pay for the school uniforms, and there would be a bus to take you into work in Harare. Perhaps, but this would be a luxury, you could afford a few small shrubs in the little garden, maybe even a small tree, grow a hedge to mark off your property, grow enough grass to dampen down the dust of the sprawling high-density commuter city. It was no surprise that South African replicas of the black US rapper groups are now so popular in the music stores. If now you've got to live a ghetto life you might as well romanticise it. But I couldn't help noticing afterwards, at the Harare Book Fair, held in the gardens between the National Gallery and the Monomotapa Hotel, street urchins looking from a distance longingly at all the books on dis-

:. 'What would it be like to be educated and have shelves of books?' haps I was myself romanticising, but that had been my background desire too – one day to have shelves of books. I had pretty much concluded that it had been Morgan Tsvangirai's too.

It had been a very interesting set of discussions. Tsvangirai himself enjoyed them and said he had seldom been pushed so hard. I hadn't been conscious of pushing, simply of trying to move him away from political soundbites and rhetoric. Certainly, by the end, he was talking freely and movingly – and personally; that is he was talking about Morgan Tsvangirai as a human being, not a political leader or political symbol. I thought I would leave the conversations therefore in chronological order to give the sense of this development. I decided in the garden too that I would not try to edit his sometimes abrupt syntax too much. Some things would have to be mildly adjusted to make the transition from spoken word to the written, but I wanted to be true to both his expression of himself and his speech cadences.

We passed by his mother and mother-in-law sitting on the verandah. His wife arrived home in the red pick-up, went inside and changed from her Western suit into the traditional wrap skirt and joined the other two women. The well-dressed and polite guards at the gates were talking among themselves and doing a good job of watching us in peripheral vision – doing their job unobtrusively. We had wandered around to the front of the garden and I noticed that my driver had not yet arrived. I said to Tsvangirai that I didn't want to keep him and I would be perfectly happy to sit on the garden bench and wait. He said he would leave me in a minute and we were both looking up, high above the bench, at the tall tree with the offending pollen.

My mind began to wander and reflect back on our conversations. Curiously I began to compare Tsvangirai with Mugabe. I thought first of the irony of Mugabe, in 1993, lecturing the Chinese leaders in Beijing. 'The question of opposition to a system is necessary and the acceptance of that is necessary for our systems to work... the party that is in power should ensure that the elections are as transparent as they can be.'[1] It was ironic because I imagined an apparatchik of Mugabe lecturing me about this book, and ironic because Mugabe was now not accepting opposition in the full and fair sense of a working democratic system. To be fair to Mugabe, I thought that he had, in his career, made at least two great speeches. I remember being stationed in Bulawayo for the 1980 independence elections. I had known the results hours before most people as the Commonwealth Observer Group had monitors at all the counting stations and, well before mobiles, we had managed to coax the Rhodesian landlines into a reliable means for exchanging information. What stunned me was not the result – although it certainly stunned Lord Soames and the British – but Mugabe's televised acceptance speech. It was a speech of reconciliation that was only eclipsed by his inauguration speech of 18 April 1980.

> If yesterday I fought you as an enemy, today you have become a friend and ally with the same national interest, loyalty, rights and duties as myself. If yesterday you hated me, you cannot avoid the love that binds you to me and me to you.

And then there had been a very ironic two sentences.

> It could never be a correct justification that because the whites oppressed us yesterday when they had power, the blacks must oppress them today because they have the power. An evil remains an evil whether practised by white against black or black against white.[2]

Or black against black for that matter. The second great speech was precisely to do with the reconciliation of black with black. At the signing of the 1992 Mozambican Peace Accord in Rome, an Accord Mugabe had greatly facilitated, he made the keynote speech.

> Today is not the day of judgement. It is the day of reconciliation. Today is not the day when we should examine who was right and who was wrong. Today is the day when we must say we are all right. Both are right in being party to the process of peace.[3]

That sense of reconciliation, and of even-handedness, seemed a long way away now. Today all the Mugabe speeches seem to be of the 'we shall put you to eternal sleep' variety. Tsvangirai saw me musing and picked up on my thought. 'Where did he go wrong?' he asked. 'You know, I once idolised that man, and when, where, did it all go wrong?' He knew of course, but it is the sort of general unbelieving question people still ask. The thing was, with Tsvangirai, that even now he could reflect and think that, if he could start over, he would have given Mugabe more space, more negotiating room, more coaxing. How could it be, I thought to myself, that a leader of the opposition should be so inclusive even of the President who persecutes him? For it is Tsvangirai who is now the one who wishes to avoid the conflictual, to set the example of dignified policy-maker rather than opposition for the sake of opposition. And it is the President who opposes the opposition, and who has let policy slip through his fingers.

Tsvangirai had said caustic words about Zimbabwean and African intellectuals. He had lamented their negativity – always establishing their critiques on blaming someone, never really completing the task of articulating an alternative except in the broadest brush strokes, calligraphing words from failed Eastern revolutions. And yet he had, from our conversations, much closer affinities with their thinking than he had ever wished to realise. He would have, starting over, concentrated far more on the African dimension. He was thinking aloud about traditional courts and procedures and their role in overall government and administration. He was passionate about Zimbabwean heritage and the under-researched long history of city civilisation in the country. Not an

African-essentialist – all things African good, all things Western necessarily imperialist – but definitely an African citizen and wanting to be a pan-Africanist. And, looking back at the ZANU(PF) intellectuals, even the most avid critics of imperialism were once modernisers, seeking 'a progressive development policy' and 'appropriate planning skills in the state sector'.[4] But it is not that he is a moderniser that really puts Tsvangirai apart from the ZANU(PF) set. Finally, the parting of the ways had been a moral one. Tsvangirai was talking in the garden about the values of university freedom. I thought to myself that this had been an inherent right of universities since their first European foundation in the 12th century. In Italy students had developed the right to establish universities and hire faculty to teach them. But, at the same time as Tsvangirai was arrested and imprisoned in 1989, the University of Zimbabwe was forcibly closed for the first time; armed soldiers and police surrounded the campus; student leaders and students generally were beaten; tear gas lingered over the campus for hours. The loss of university freedom then seemed to presage a later more general loss of freedom. Tsvangirai left ZANU(PF) and felt betrayed by Mugabe precisely because the moral quality of freedom was being undermined.

After I left Zimbabwe the MDC announced it would not contest the March 2005 parliamentary elections unless certain conditions were met. Tsvangirai had hinted at this in our conversations, but I was dismayed. It was a very high-risk strategy. It was true that much African and other international opinion was in favour of genuinely fair elections. In a speech that had greatly heartened Tsvangirai, Kofi Annan had said:

> This new spirit of democratic empowerment in Africa must find a home in every African country. For that to happen, politics must be inclusive, and a careful institutional balance must be preserved – including regular free and fair elections, a credible opposition whose role is respected, an independent judiciary which upholds the rule of law, a free and independent press, effective civilian control over the military, and a vibrant civil society.

And, at the SADC summit in Mauritius on 17 August 2004, the host prime minister, Paul Berenger, as if speaking directly to Mugabe who was in attendance, said:

> Really free and fair elections mean not only an independent electoral commission, but also freedom of assembly and absence of physical harassment by the police or any other entity, freedom of the press and access to national radio and television, and external and credible observation of the whole electoral process.[5]

Political observers were certain these comments had been rehearsed with Thabo Mbeki who was also in attendance. And this was where Mbeki's sense of pragmatism was stronger than his sense of pan-Africanism. South Africa was simply not able to advance as it wished within a region that was closely interlinked, and in which what had been a key part of the jigsaw, Zimbabwe, now no longer fitted economically. And, more importantly, Zimbabwe's condition simply frustrated southern Africa's links with the economically powerful and necessary outside world. Berenger continued:

> With free and fair elections due in Zimbabwe at the beginning of next year we can already start preparing for the normalisation of relations between SADC, the European Union and the US.[6]

The MDC announcement of a boycott on 25 August 2004 was greeted with jubilation by ZANU(PF). The *Herald* quoted the University of Zimbabwe's Professor Claude Mararike as saying, 'the party is employing this as a defence mechanism to create an excuse in advance after noticing that they are unable to win the battle'.[7] The MDC strategy seemed to be one of throwing the ball back into the court of SADC – a 'you've said this, now make it happen' type of challenge. The MDC's Paul Themba Nyathi had said: 'Until there are tangible signs the government is prepared to enforce the SADC protocols on elections, the national executive has today decided to suspend participation in all forms of elections in Zimbabwe.'[8]

Whether SADC will, or can, pressure Mugabe to make more concessions will certainly be known by the time this book is released. Certainly, the world at large and, now, even Africa wants free and fair elections in Zimbabwe, and the initial ZANU(PF) response betrays its parochialism rather than its pan-Africanist solidarity. Africa might want to be more African, but Africa is also wanting to be more democratic. Moreover, it seems that even ZANU(PF) might understand but wishes to defy this. Mararike went on to say that the MDC may have been receiving funds from Obasanjo's Nigeria. Having said all that, Maraike is not without a point. The MDC has been weakened, there are – despite Tsvangirai's reassuring words – serious fissures within the party. Its organisational base and capacity have been eroded. There are many diplomatic observers who believe that, even if ZANU(PF) implemented all the SADC conditions, the MDC would not be able to win the parliamentary elections. My own feeling at the end of August is that ZANU(PF) will not wish to satisfy SADC. It not only wants to win but, even if it thinks it can win, it has now developed a culture of ensuring that it wins at all costs. It will not resist itself. But, if that happens and the MDC does not contest the elections, what will happen to Tsvangirai? Will he then retire?

Morgan Tsvangirai has come a long way from his 'streets of Belgrade' enthusiasm. The last thing he now wants for Zimbabwe is violence and a lack of democratic change. He has lost a huge amount of naivety from the time I first interviewed him in 2000. But his Presidential chance may not come.

At one stage in 2001, US and UK embassy officials in Harare confided to me that their feeling was that the MDC was not fully prepared for government. What they wanted to see was Morgan Tsvangirai as President, so that the country's leadership could be renewed and given energy – as well as a more inclusive and democratic impulse. But they also wanted to see a ZANU(PF) majority in parliament, to ensure continuity in government institutions and sufficient technocratic command of key positions. In their terms, even if the MDC contests – and then wins – the March elections, it will be the exact inverse of their favoured scenario: a ZANU(PF) President and an MDC parliament. The Americans and the British have been frequently wrong in their judgements, but I had, in the conversations with Tsvangirai, consistently pushed him on the calibre of his front bench, and he was admitting that many people had been placed in the wrong positions. Perhaps everything is ready now, perhaps he has finally developed the party to become an actual government.

Morgan Tsvangirai and I were still in his garden. We were standing underneath his beautiful problematic tree. I joked, 'at least in this garden you can't be bugged'. I made to sit down on the bench. He smiled ruefully and said, 'that is the bench where Ari Ben-Manashe sat'.

He explained that it had been in the early days of their relationship. He didn't want to talk about it too much, but he was clearly rueing the fact that he had taken into his trust a man who was there to deceive, entrap and betray him. He said, 'he was my guest here', as if to ask how someone could receive hospitality and then betray his host. I looked up for Tsvangirai's eyes, but they were still looking at the bench. It was the only sign he gave in all our hours together of what the sword hanging over him, the treason verdict, the possibility of a hangman's noose, had done to him.

I remained silent as he made his farewells and went into his house. I heard him talking with the women on the verandah. I sat on the bench and tried to imagine what it had all been like, shuffling my notes and trying to repackage my tapes in the right order. I heard the distinctive needing-a-good-tune-up sound of my car coming up the street. I thought, very sadly, how much the country had declined and how unnecessary it had all been. I thought of all my Zimbabwean friends and the hard lives they now had to lead. I thought of those among them who had died of HIV/AIDS. I thought of those who had heroically waited to vote, but it had been a useless wait. And would they wait again? Would they have the chance to wait again?

I waved goodbye to the guards. They had gotten to smile at me by now. My driver, who after some years of carting me around knows me very well, saw me silent and left me silent. I was thinking: yes, he will need to be surrounded by good advisors and ministers, but he knows that; yes, he still has many flaws, but he knows that too; but, yes, he has so many positive qualities of idealism, hope, and vision. He may be closer to his hero, Mandela, than even he suspects. Discussion by discussion, Morgan Tsvangirai had become more open, more human – less cautious and, paradoxically, more obviously and naturally presidential. A man of many aspects. What lingered as I walked away from the last interview, however, was the thread that had run through each of the perspectives he had articulated, the feature that had defined the man: Morgan Tsvangirai exemplified the virtues, the shouldering of responsibility and the growing vision of a citizen of contemporary Africa.

Notes

1. *Sunday Times* (Harare), 9 May 1993.
2. Cited in the *Journal of Southern African Studies*, 30:2, 2004, p. 393.
3. Cited in Cameron Hume, *Ending Mozambique's War*, Washington DC: US Institute of Peace, 1994, p. 137.
4. Ibbo Mandaza, 'Introduction', in Ibbo Mandaza (ed.), *The Political Economy of Transition 1980-1986*, Dakar: CODESRIA, 1987, pp. 17-18.
5. Address to the African Union Summit, Addis Ababa, 6 July 2004.
6. *The Guardian* (London), 18 August 2004.
7. 27 August 2004.
8. *The Guardian*, 26 August 2004.

The Twisting
& Turning Road Forwards

In this chapter I will try to update the career of Morgan Tsvangirai. I have not spoken at length with him since the 2005 elections, but we have exchanged messages and his have always been, characteristically, and even when I was writing critically of him, full of good cheer. If he were judged on nothing but human spirit he would be ahead of us all. He has his own human failings, however, and some of these have translated into political judgements. There were a lot of wrong calls along the way to the Prime Ministership. I want to remain critical of him, not simply validate him, but make it clear that I admire him. These are cards I place openly on the table. There is far too much blind or blinkered support or demonisation, pure and without nuance, when it comes to African politics. People and situations are complex. All exonerations and condemnations have mitigating circumstances. Cases for the defence can be as powerful as those for the prosecution. The last thing Africa needs is more black and white. Morgan Tsvangirai is a vexed, difficult, contradictory, courageous, idealistic and determined person. It takes a lot to absorb all there is about him. Many of his closest lieutenants broke away from him, unable or unwilling to stomach the combination any more. Thabo Mbeki of South Africa took literally years to come to a balanced view of him. Robert Mugabe has his own ambivalent views of him. When Tsvangirai comes to London, the Foreign Office really are uncertain how best to handle him. They want to support him, but think he makes things difficult for them. The post-mortems, late at night in King Charles Street, overlooking the sleeping pelicans of St. James' Park, are not as straightforward as ZANU(PF) might have imagined.

The 2005 Parliamentary elections

These were important elections insofar as they marked a radical departure from previous practice by ZANU(PF) – and this was the careful planning of centrally coordinated rigging. Rigging had been largely localised and *ad hoc* up to this point, with low intensity intimidation being preferred as a device *before* elections, rather than rigging as a device *after* the polls had closed. Even so, ZANU(PF) was sufficiently confident that previous polling patterns would be repeated – giving it victory – that the plan to rig was established as a fall-back mechanism. Having said that, rigging was not the only reason why ZANU(PF) won the 2005 elections. The MDC made many mistakes. The pattern – of ZANU(PF) intimidation and confidence, rigging as a default plan if things looked like going wrong, and MDC mistakes – was repeated in 2008.

The key mistakes made by the MDC were four-fold. Firstly, the MDC lost one of its most important city seats, Harare South. The party had not been helped by boundary changes, but it had also imposed an unpopular candidate, removing one who had much local support. This was a mistake, as was the failure, nationally, to contest the boundary changes – which were all approved in a legal manner.

Secondly, the MDC held onto most – but not all – its rural seats in the two Matabeleland provinces. There had clearly not been a significant enough outreach either to the rural areas in general or, in particular, those that had predominantly Ndebele populations. The east-west divide would return to haunt the MDC, but the insecurity of its only real rural base helped cement the image of the MDC as an urban formation. Whenever ZANU(PF) rigged rural votes, therefore, it was able to look credible.

Thirdly, the MDC would have secured a higher share of the vote, but many people were turned away at the polling stations for not having registered properly beforehand, or for turning up at the wrong constituency. The MDC had not run any properly coordinated voter education campaign or registration drive.

Fourthly, particularly in the rural areas, with the strategic role played by village chiefs and headmen, ZANU(PF) was able to channel misinformation to the voters, for example, that the transparent ballot boxes that conformed to African Union regulations would reveal how an individual had voted; that the dye used on fingers to mark someone who had voted would betray fingerprints on a ballot paper and, again, allow a vote to be traceable – but MDC party agents, both leading up to the poll and at the polling stations themselves did nothing to counter such suggestions. Often they gave no advice at all to voters and seemed, at times, not to know what they were meant to be doing.

Even so, the election should have been a much closer run thing than it was. Fearing it might not achieve a sufficient electoral victory, and would therefore have to depend on the President's appointed MPs to achieve a sustainable parliamentary majority, ZANU(PF) decided to wheel out its default rigging plan. It was very clear *when* additional ZANU(PF) votes materialised but, to this day, no one really has the forensic detail as to how it is done. I'm sure I have a much more accurate impression of how it is done than the US State Department, with whom I have shared notes, but there is nothing that amounts to hard evidence.

Voting was heaviest in the morning. By the afternoon, at the vast majority of polling stations, the queues had dwindled to trickles. On national television, Ibbo Mandaza was saying, as early as 2pm on voting day, that the contest would be settled by the votes already cast. This was said against the official throughput figures that were also broadcast. The registered electorate that would be expected to vote simply wasn't that much larger. When counting was underway, however, and the broadcast of results had already begun, there was an abrupt announcement that the release of results was being suspended. When it resumed some hours later, there seemed to be a huge upswing in late votes cast. There was often no symmetry between early progress figures on throughput and final votes. There was sometimes even no symmetry between overall voting totals and the numbers of votes accorded each candidate in any one constituency. In the late announcements, the lion's share of the new votes went to ZANU(PF). The interesting thing is that this should not be seen as rigging across the board. It was certainly centrally coordinated, but it concentrated on just enough key seats to ensure that ZANU(PF) had a comfortable electoral majority – and, of course, an even stronger parliamentary one with the addition of the appointed MPs. The aim was not to destroy the MDC as an opposition force, but to ensure it was large enough to display as evidence of Zimbabwean 'democracy', and small enough effectively to be regulated within the institutions of parliament. The MDC won 41 seats and claimed it should have been 62 – meaning a theft of more than 20. My own estimate is that the theft was in the order of ten to twelve. Even so, rigging had been shown to work and to be forensically untraceable. The MDC has never sought to uncover how this is done. In any nationally coordinated exercise of this sort, huge numbers of people would be involved – and Harare is a notoriously gossipy town with much interaction between people from different parties. The lack of loose gossip, or the lack of pattern in loose gossip, is a worrying indication of how lacking in depth the MDC intelligence capacity then was.

The split in the MDC

If a party leader's judgement and capacity may be fairly reflected in how his party performs in an election, and how well it *prepares* its performance, then there would have been question marks over Morgan Tsvangirai. To be fair, ZANU(PF) had gone out of its way to destabilise him with treason charges before the 2005 elections but, also to be honest, the MDC performance in 2005 – rigging notwithstanding

– was simply not outstanding. The party seemed hopeful but weary. Having said that, the critical criterion by which a party leader is normally judged is in whether he has a party to lead – let alone one which he leads to victory. The split in the MDC raised even more question marks over Tsvangirai.

The contretemps within the MDC towards the end of 2005, over whether or not to contest the newly recreated senate, merely brought to a head a long-simmering discontent within the upper echelons of the party that Morgan Tsvangirai often bypassed the official apparatus of the party – including its executive – and operated through a parallel structure. To be fair to Tsvangirai, in moments of emergency, rapid and unilateral decisions had to be made. That is a mark of leadership and, in such cases, bureaucracy is not. The problem was two-fold. Firstly, he used the parallel structure even when there was no immediate emergency and, secondly, having made a unilateral decision, he would often vacillate and change his mind – leaving confusion in his wake. Even his friends began to comment on an enigmatic character trait of decisive indecisiveness. He still had great popular support but, to many party seniors, he was not behaving like a good leader. The angry energies generated under such conditions came to a head when, against Tsvangirai's advice, the MDC National Council voted 33 to 31 that the party should contest the senate elections. It was a close vote, but a democratic decision. Tsvangirai, however, elided the truth of what had happened. He announced to the press that the National Council had been deadlocked. Now, in fact, there had been two spoilt ballots – and Tsvangirai regarded them as being votes against entering the senatorial contest. So, in the Tsvangirai version, the vote had been tied 33 and 33 and, on the basis of his own casting vote, he said the MDC would not enter the contest. Pandemonium erupted in the party. Despite huge mediation efforts between the pro and anti-Tsvangirai factions – chiefly led by Brian Raftopoulos – the MDC split. Some of Tsvangirai's hitherto closest lieutenants left him – as did a very large part of the Matabeleland-based MDC.

Whether the senate issue also brought to a head other seemingly structural fault-lines within the MDC – the east-west/Shona-Ndebele divide being only one – such as an intellectual/trade union divide, is another set of questions. All such questions, however, devolved themselves to a central one to do with leadership. A good leader is meant to unite people, then lead them. If he can't unite them, he persuades them that the goal, and the strategy towards that goal, are powerful enough for them to pretend to be united. If all divisions are in some way represented on a council or an executive, except in dire emergencies that body should not be bypassed.

Having said all that, the emergence of Arthur Mutambara as leader of the breakaway MDC was more important than many think. He was plucked from obscurity in South Africa, having never led any political organisation since his student days. He had clearly been a brilliant scholar and businessman – but was hardly a tested leader. But his intellectual qualities allowed Mugabe, under the fractious talks that passed for Thabo Mbeki's mediation in 2008, to find an entry-point for engagement with some part of the MDC, some part of the opposition. If it had been left to Mbeki trying to bring only Mugabe and Tsvangirai together, nothing would have happened. The person who could have been the 'spoiler' became the wedge that opened both sides towards an accommodation – not that he knew he was doing that. Before then, however, the three parties – ZANU(PF), MDC-Mutambara and MDC-Tsvangirai – had to fight the 2008 combined presidential and parliamentary elections. ZANU(PF), given its own strength, was convinced it would win without too much effort, without the need for too much intimidation beforehand, and with no default plan to rig ready to go at a moment's notice. In any case, it would have been harder to rig. The growing number of African Union requirements – such as the posting of results on the wall of each and every polling station – meant that a nationally-coordinated rig required control of a huge number of variables. ZANU(PF) thought, in any case, it was going to 'walk it' against a divided and dispirited opposition with serious questions over the leadership experience of Mutambara and over the leadership of Tsvangirai. The fact that ZANU(PF) had bankrupted the nation's electorate seemed not to have crossed its mind. And, for once, things began going the way of the opposition. ZANU(PF) itself split – although the split never grew to the proportions anticipated. But the departure of Simba Makoni meant, or should have meant, some accrual of advantage to the two MDCs.

The 2008 elections

Morgan Tsvangirai failed – through obstinacy and a refusal to concede sufficient space to Mutambara's MDC – to form a grand alliance against Mugabe and ZANU(PF). In the end, it was Mutambara who stood down from the presidential race in favour of Makoni – but there was no outreach from Tsvangirai himself to Makoni. This was, all the while, in the face of an astonishingly inept ZANU(PF) campaign. Its advertising, whether on television, in newspapers, or on hoardings was lacklustre, poorly designed and often simply shoddy. Tsvangirai's MDC television advertisements, as in 2005, were so slick that they resonated with an urban electorate – and meant nothing to a rural one which, in any case, had little access to television. But the contrast was there. Almost as if at the last moment, ZANU(PF) realised how last-generation its advertising was, and glossy billboards of Robert Mugabe vowing defence of Zimbabwe appeared on the city streets. He wore a beautiful suit and, clenching his fist, stood guard over the radiant blue and green of the Victoria Falls. They were, almost of course, the Zambian side of the Falls.

But ZANU(PF), right until almost the last, was sure it would win. Opinion polls suggested it would. But it didn't. It was only towards the final few days of the campaign that the scent of a pending upset infiltrated the nostrils of all parties. Mugabe had been told, in private session but point-blank to his face, by village elders in the Mutare area that great dissatisfaction had grown over ZANU(PF)'s economic performance. All the blaming of outsiders, and all the election gifts of tractors and food would not deflect their criticism. Those brave enough to say this in other areas also said it. Mugabe himself was psychologically prepared for what was to come. Which is why, when it came, for a brief moment at least he was prepared to stand down.

As the polls closed and counting began, SABC (South African Broadcasting Corporation) estimated an MDC victory of 52 per cent, with the bulk of that going to the Tsvangirai faction. I had the victory margin firmly at 56 per cent. Early MDC projections were higher than that, based – apparently – on the cellphone photographs of election results posted outside individual polling stations. Later, the MDC would backtrack but still claim victory at slightly over 50 per cent. A year after the elections, some 'informed' gossip in Harare suggested that it was in fact 57 per cent. It was at this point that the mettle of statesmanship was tested in both Tsvangirai and Mbeki. As soon as the trend became clear, a delegation of senior ZANU(PF) personnel (the 'doves' of the party) met with Tsvangirai and his lieutenants, bargaining for immunities (which, immediately, the South Africans, acting on behalf of the US State Department, guaranteed), and for the MDC-dominated cabinet to include a minority of ZANU(PF) ministers (South Africa also encouraged this). Tsvangirai and his lieutenants refused. I think they should have accepted.

Some few days later, when the ZANU(PF) politburo met, after early progress by the doves, the 'hawks' rallied and insisted upon a run-off. Mugabe, ever the good party-man, recovered his sense of determination and agreed to fight, and then began the protracted counting down of the opposition's vote. The plan to do this existed, but had now to be revised, both because of time elapsed and public expectation of a change in government, and because African Union polling procedures and a flock of official observers had made such rigging a painstaking process. Those constituencies with clear photographic evidence of the results had to be left relatively alone. Those with blurred or no photographic evidence had to have the results 'reassigned' – but in a careful manner. The votes for parliament were going to be, by and large, conceded, so the prize at stake was the presidential vote. This had not to differ too remarkably from the parliamentary vote; it had to be a rig that was diffused across a wide national catchment and, something under-remarked, votes had to be subtracted not only from Tsvangirai but, with less risk of backlash, from Makoni. It took weeks. It was an exercise in intelligence and mathematics, sleights of hand as transparent and sealed boxes were cloned, and secrecy so as not to allow overmuch suspicion to form in recognisable patterns. There were still some residual observers looking on. When the 'results' were finally announced, and a run-off declared, it was clear what had happened but also clear that it had happened carefully.

The point is that, if Mbeki had thrown his weight behind the doves at the critical politburo meeting, the fiasco of what followed would not have occurred. But his distaste for Tsvangirai clouded what should have been his insistence on respecting the democratic will. Also, he would have known that a rig was in progress during the long weeks of 'counting' that followed.

Having been once bitten, ZANU(PF) took to the second round with a reversion to violence as the key conditioning agent. Even Mbeki became alarmed by its scale and pervasiveness. What was already a travesty had become a brutal mockery. During this time, Tsvangirai made many mistakes. They included not spending enough time in the country; leaving the MDC-faithful demoralised and without leadership; seeking refuge in the Dutch embassy, in a staged effort to demonstrate the threat of assassination (as if assassins worked only at night, when he was a clearer target at his daylight open rallies); paying too much attention to the advice of personnel from Washington-based foundations; relying on the support of the Botswanan president without seeking to widen such high-level endorsement; and, finally, in withdrawing from the election just days before the polling on the grounds of advice from his party activists which, in fact, had never been properly sampled. I regret that this second electoral round saw Tsvangirai demonstrate exactly what leadership was *not*. I understand the pressures upon him. I think he fluffed it and am prepared to say it.

But the violence had been so palpable that few in the outside world found the Mugabe 'victory' convincing. Thabo Mbeki was instructed by his peers to sort the sorry situation out. Behind all the rhetoric of support for Mugabe lay profound disquiet. This sort of 'election' could only have knock-on effects for the rest of Africa. Presidents supported Mugabe. He was also the last thing they needed.

What Thabo had always wanted

Mbeki, with the shadow of Jacob Zuma now looming over his own shoulder, set to work. There was an irony that he was trying to 'sort' a stolen election when he himself was about to be deposed in a non-electoral fashion. His enemies would say this was just. That would be slightly unfair. The Mbeki view, apart from bad chemistry with Tsvangirai – which now did slowly start to ease – was that he really did think that both Tsvangirai and the MDC were unprepared for government. He was particularly alarmed by Tsvangirai's penchant for prevarication and vacillation. Those who left him to form an MDC that came to be led by Mutambara thought exactly the same thing. But Mbeki's was an alarm that had developed early and, from 2002, he had formed a plan in which Tsvangirai would be vice-president. Vice president, prime minister – the use of the prime minister's position as a compromise had been an innovation from Kofi Annan in the Kenyan crisis – Mbeki's sense was that Tsvangirai would make a good number two. Never mind what the electorate might have been trying to say. To be fair, he also had in mind what ZANU(PF) would do if it lost power – especially the hawks and their military firepower. Mbeki was certainly not going to send South African tanks across the border to sort out *that* sort of thing. So his rubric was inclusiveness and the sub-text was an apprenticeship for Tsvangirai; his model was both what he had earlier accomplished by way of power-sharing in the Democratic Republic of Congo, and what Kofi Annan had accomplished in Kenya.

Although the Kenyan prime minister advised Tsvangirai by phone constantly in the negotiations that followed, it was finally Tsvangirai's own decision to accept the compromise with its outline distribution of ministerial portfolios. And, despite all protestations, and Tsvangirai's backtracking in the face of dissent from his closest lieutenants, he probably *did* agree Home Affairs to be a ZANU(PF) portfolio. Tsvangirai's changing of his mind in the face of pressure afterwards, Mbeki told his peers, was just another example of the man's vacillation. From agreement, through arguments and further compromise, to activation of the power-sharing government, through initial huge difficulties of mutual accommodation, through Susan Tsvangirai's tragic death, to a period of relatively stable but still fractious cooperation, we arrive at the present moment. Everything is completely unsatisfactory. Everything is as good as it could be, given the circumstances. Some conditions of life are beginning to improve.

The highly conditional way forward

In a very real sense, Morgan Tsvangirai has never been without controversy. Even the birth of the MDC left many in the NCA aggrieved. It seemed to them a pre-emptive move and one made without any reflection on the merits of change via civil society compared with change from oppositional politics and a trust in electoral democracy. It would seem fair to suggest that he has been at his best in two key periods. The first was, having embraced the route of an opposition party, his performance as party leader in the early days, probably right up to the 2005 elections – although discontents within the MDC were no secret well before then – when he was internationally recognised as courageous, sustained, principled and determined. Exemplary. After 2005, he seemed to lose his way and never really recovered his poise and balance, even his nerve, until he finally became prime minister. In this sense, Thabo Mbeki is to be thanked. He leveraged the post in which Tsvangirai could prove himself and shine. The first year of the prime ministership has been a triumph – albeit against a background of tensions, calculated acts of sabotage, threats, selective harassments and sustained reluctant cooperation or no cooperation at all. Tsvangirai's demeanour throughout all this has been statesmanlike. Even in London's Foreign Office, whether looking out at the Queen's pelicans or not, and whether he was fully understood or not, there is agreement that he is becoming a class act. Even Thabo Mbeki has kind words to say about him these days. And there would seem to be a tentative but genuine rapprochement between Tsvangirai and Mugabe. This is in personal terms. These days, Mugabe is as much a prisoner of his hawks as he is their leader. In Mugabe, Tsvangirai deals with a condition of symbiosis. It seems that rich and powerful men and women cannot be satisfied with possessions and bling that make Hollywood stars seem infantile in what they have accumulated. More begets the urge towards even more, forever more. At least Hollywood stars affect learning by having mansions filled with bookshelves and art. The palaces and mansions of Borrowdale Brook are all marble staircases and obviously homes to show–offs and dunces. All this in the name of a liberation ideology, so that a self-conceit blends with a self-deceit – as the ideologues liberate the economy for themselves. There is a pathological condition in Zimbabwe and, here, it is Tsvangirai who is the sane man.

What must he do? He cannot increase the reserves of US dollars and SA rands by magic. He cannot improve the nation's productive economic base without huge expenditures. Restoration is always harder than assisted degeneration. Assisted restoration requires greater flows of international investment than he has right now. The West is reluctant to increase these flows without political conditions. The first is an obvious one as far as the West is concerned. Gideon Gono, with his one honorary and his one false doctorate, must go. The West will not help rebuild an economy when a key economic governor is considered part of the pathology of kleptomania. But the West can only insist on this through Tsvangirai. It is not talking to Mugabe. And the West will not take the risk, at time of writing, to frontload its financial assistance as inducement that Gono should go. The stand-off is over the sense of ultimatum coming from the West, and this is another tactical mistake in London and Washington. Nor will it easily reconsider the possibility of talking directly to Mugabe – who is, for Mbeki's better or worse, president. But it can't expect Tsvangirai to persuade Mugabe at least to attempt to curtail his hawks and their financier without giving Tsvangirai some means of leverage. That means money, and that also means being nice to Mugabe's sense of dignity. He might deserve to be a pariah, but he reacts badly to being treated like a pariah. Right now, behind the scenes, the immunities deal that the British are prepared to lay on the table is that even the worst and richest hawks can feel free from international retribution and prosecution – provided they remain in Zimbabwe. To that might plausibly be added the SADC region and, to that, might conditionally be added a great deal of Africa and some other parts of the Third World. But Harrods in Knightsbridge and Fifth Avenue in New York are off-limits. It is, in the farcical way historical eras always end, coming down to the right, having first stolen money, to spend it on bling.

And the historical era *is* ending. Even Robert Mugabe is not immortal. When he dies, an era will begin to appreciate it has no cause to remain in existence in its present form. What Tsvangirai needs to do is to engage very visibly and noisily with the doves in ZANU(PF), get Simba Makoni back into the political mainstream, propagate Arthur Mutambara and Welshman Ncube as God's answer to humanity's invention of sliced bread, and basically set about reinventing not just Zimbabwean politics but political society. When the hawks realise there is no place left for them to perch, they will retire at last to their well-feathered nests. Their children will use their families' ill-gotten gains as capital to grow legitimate businesses and these will, perhaps perversely – but this is also how the USA grew – help the growth of Zimbabwe. Tsvangirai has got to have a sense of history that is based on the idea of a long cycle – and help all this along. Can the man who, at times, barely had the MDC under his control do all this? Has he grown in stature and capacity to such an extent?

Probably not. And it's hardly his fault. Politics in Zimbabwe is notoriously parochial and self-regarding – narrow-minded in terms of its time and space. However, it was Tsvangirai who was elected – no matter what the power-sharing deal says – by a margin of 56 or 57%. People want him to carry their hopes into the future. Most of the world wants him to succeed. What I have tried to say in this additional chapter is that, under the weight of all these expectations, there is a man who will try very hard – but who has his own frail shoulders. I have not made a saint of him, not even an Atlas. I hope I have not criticised him too much or too unfairly. Probably no one could have done for Zimbabwe what he has. I do mean to say that Zimbabwe has a very human being for its prime minister, and I wish him well with all my heart.

The first edition of this book portrayed a Tsvangirai who was more intellectually curious and better read, and certainly more thoughtful than many believed. It portrayed a modernist and a moderniser. It portrayed a natural humanist and a man who was stoic and courageous. It portrayed a man who regretted both his betrayal by Ben Manashe and, inflected in this, his own naivety in trusting such men. It portrayed someone who could not bear to cut down a beautiful tree, despite the hay fever it caused him. I found that wonderful. So I shall conclude this second edition by reference to something that may be just romantic. The French writer, Jean Giono, wrote a lovely novella called *The Man who Planted Trees*. It was a gentle tale of a peasant who revitalised an entire devastated region, simply by daily, for years, planting trees. Not cutting them down is the first exemplary step.